Ambassadors on Mission:

The Priority of Prayer and Proclamation

Dan R. Crawford

Published by
Hannibal Books
PO Box 461592
Garland, Texas 75046-1592
Copyright Dan Crawford 2009
All Rights Reserved
Printed in the United States of America
by Lightning Source, LaVergne, TN
Cover design by Dennis Davidson
Except where otherwise indicated, all Scripture taken from the Holy Bible,
New King James Version, copyright 1979, 1980, 1982, and 1988
by Thomas Nelson Publishers
ISBN 978-1-934749-70-8
Library of Congress Control Number: 2009942753
To order more copies of this book see order form on page 121

Dedicated

to those who have taught me the priority of being prepared for prayer and proclamation

CONTENTS

Ambassadors for Christ

In my younger years one of the most exciting activities at church was the Sword Drill, later called the Bible Drill. I participated in this competitive event through an organization called Royal Ambassadors, whose motto was taken from 2 Corinthians 5:20, *we are ambassadors for Christ.* At that point in my life I had never heard the term *spiritual warfare* and had no idea that the enjoyable commands of the Sword Drill—*Attention! Draw Swords! Charge!*—were military in nature. Sooner or later believers begin to realize that the Christian life is a battleground, not a playground.

Lately I have begun to comprehend a key to understanding this increasingly popular subject—namely, Christians are not primarily warriors by nature but ambassadors on mission. Warriors fight and defend their country—often in other countries. Ambassadors represent their king in another kingdom. Warriors are military. Ambassadors are diplomatic. Nevertheless, ambassadors, while representing their king, become engaged in warfare.

The Apostle Paul, who wrote most of the biblical material on spiritual warfare, was an ambassador. He lived in a day in which military terminology was widely used. He lived in an empire that was built and preserved by military power. But Paul was not a military man, even though he wrote with the military terminology of his day as he implored Timothy to *endure hardship as a good soldier of Jesus Christ* (2 Tim. 2:3) and assured him that he, himself, had *fought the good fight* (2 Tim. 4:7).

The scriptural basis for this book is found in Paul's writing in Ephesians 6:10-20:

Finally, my brethren, be strong in the Lord and in the power of His might. Put on the whole armor of God, that you may be able to stand against the wiles of the devil. For we do not wrestle against flesh and blood, but against principalities, against powers, against the rulers of the darkness of this age, against spiritual hosts of wickedness in the heavenly places. Therefore take up the whole armor of God, that you may be able to withstand in the evil day, and having done all, to stand. Stand therefore, having girded your waist with truth, having put on the breastplate of righteousness, and having shod your feet with the preparation of the gospel of peace; above all, taking the shield of faith with which you will be able to quench all the fiery darts of the wicked one. And take the helmet of salvation, and the sword of the Spirit, which is the word of God; praying always with all prayer and supplication in the Spirit, being watchful to this end with all perseverance and supplication for all the saints—and for me, that utterance may be given to me, that I may open my mouth boldly to make known the mystery of the gospel, for which I am an ambassador in chains; that in it I may speak boldly, as I ought to speak.

Besides the passage in Ephesians 6:10-20 other warfare references in Paul's letters are as follows:

- Romans 13:12—*put on the armor of light.*
- 1 Corinthians 9:7—*Who ever goes to war at his own expense?*
- 1 Corinthians 14:8—*if a trumpet makes an uncertain sound, who will prepare himself for battle?*
- 1 Corinthians 16:9—*a great and effective door has opened to me, and there are many adversaries.*
- 2 Corinthians 6:7—*by the armor of righteousness on the right hand and on the left . . .*
- 2 Corinthians 10:3-4—*For though we walk in the flesh, we do not war according to the flesh. For the weapons of our warfare are not carnal but mighty in God for the pulling down of strongholds . . .*
- Philippians 2:25—*Epaphroditus, my brother, fellow worker, and fellow soldier . . .*
- Colossians 2:15—*Having disarmed principalities and powers . . .*
- 1 Thessalonians 5:8—*putting on the breastplate of faith and love, and as a helmet the hope of salvation.*
- 1 Timothy 1:18—*that by them you may wage the good warfare . . .*

In contrast to these warfare references in Paul's writings he referred to himself 17 times as an apostle, 14 times as a servant, slave or a prisoner, 12 times as a teacher or an exhorter, 13 times as an intercessor, 17 times as a minister, five times as a missionary, and 38 times as a preacher or edifier. Clearly Paul's vision of himself was not primarily as a defender under attack but as an ambassador on mission. He was an ambassador who took on the roles of apostle, servant, exhorter, intercessor, minister, missionary, and preacher.

When Paul pictured the Christian life as warfare, he pictured Christians—even as they were representing Him—defending the gospel against the enemies of Christ. To the church at Corinth he wrote, *Now then, we are ambassadors for Christ, as though God were pleading through us: we implore you on Christ's behalf, be reconciled to God* (2 Cor. 5:20). In the passage often referred to as containing the *weapons of our warfare*, Paul wrote, *I am an ambassador in chains* (Eph. 6:20).

In so identifying himself and his readers, Paul was echoing Old Testament writers. The writer of the Proverbs exclaimed, *a faithful ambassador brings health* (Prov. 13:17). Isaiah wrote, *The ambassadors of peace shall weep bitterly* (Isa. 33:7). Jeremiah wrote, *an ambassador has been sent to the nations . . . rise up to battle!* (Jer. 49:14).

Many who preach, teach and write on the subject of spiritual warfare do so from the perspective that we are warriors, fighting Satan, striving to win a battle. The following chapters are written from the perspective that we primarily are ambassadors, who in the activity of representing our King in another kingdom get caught in the crossfire of the battle being waged *in the heavenly places* and thus are in need of spiritual armor. The warfare is not ours, except that we represent our Lord, Who already has claimed ultimate victory.

We are not on a seek-and-destroy assignment where Satan is concerned. We are following a command to *"make disciples of all the nations"* (Mt. 28:19). To the degree we are effective in following our great commission, we will encounter spiritual conflict. When we are effectively on mission is when we find we are under attack.

This book is based on the premise that the spiritual armor and Paul's instructions in Ephesians 6:10-17 find a purpose in verses 18-20. When Paul has completed his instructions on warfare and his description of the spiritual armor, he states without a break in his thoughts, *praying always*. The object of this intercessory prayer is Paul and his bold *utterance* of the *mystery of the gospel*—in other words, his proclamation. To state this in another way, one purpose of spiritual armor and spiritual instruction is to prepare the Christian ambassador to stand firm against Satan in the practice of intercessory prayer for the proclamation of the gospel.

David Martyn Lloyd-Jones, a British pastor and writer who excelled in expository preaching, wrote of this connection:

> What is the relationship of this "praying always" to what the Apostle has been dealing with hitherto? . . . Surely it is that this "praying in the spirit" is something we have to do, and to keep on doing, in connection with the use of the whole armor, and indeed with the whole of our position as Christians in conflict with the world and the flesh and the devil. Paul says, "Take these various separate parts of the armor and put them on, and put them on carefully, and use them in every way described . . . but in addition to all of that, always and at all times and in every circumstance keep on praying."[1]

So the priority message of Ephesians 6:10-20 is neither spiritual armor nor warfare instructions but prayer and proclamation, which will be enhanced by spiritual armor and warfare instructions.

Thus, this is another look at spiritual warfare but from a slightly different perspective—the perspective of an ambassador needing to be prepared in the priorities of prayer and proclamation.

[1]David Martyn Lloyd-Jones, *The Christian Soldier: An Exposition of Ephesians 6:10 to 20*. Grand Rapids: Baker Book House, 1977, 337-38.

Chapter 1

SPIRITUAL WARFARE, PRAYER, AND PROCLAMATION

Finally, my brethren . . .

The New Testament church was birthed and commissioned to make disciples to the very ends of the earth. As soon as they began to fulfill this Great Commission, believers began to encounter spiritual warfare. Consider the following examples:

- Acts 5—Satan attacked the church from within through the prominent family of Ananias and Sapphira.
- Acts 8—God was moved to separate, through heavy persecution, the church in Jerusalem from its Jewish comfort zone.
- Acts 13—Satan's representative was humiliated, defeated, and blinded through the ministry of Paul.
- Acts 16—Warfare was fought over the demonized slave girl of Philippi.
- Acts 19—Warfare was waged between the Spirit of God and the evil spirits associated with some Jewish exorcists in Ephesus.

Nor did these encounters with evil end in Acts. Consider what else Paul wrote concerning spiritual warfare:

- 1 Corinthians 9:26-27—*Therefore I run thus: not with uncertainty. Thus I fight: not as one who beats the air. But I discipline my body and bring it into subjection, lest, when I have preached to others, I myself should become disqualified.*
- 2 Corinthians 10:3-5—*For though we walk in the flesh, we do not war according to the flesh. For the weapons of our warfare are not carnal but mighty in God for pulling down strongholds, casting down arguments and every high thing that exalts itself against the knowledge of God, bringing every thought into captivity to the obedience of Christ.*
- 1 Thessalonians 5:8—*But let us who are of the day be sober, putting on the breastplate of faith and love, as a helmet the hope of salvation.*
- 1 Timothy 1:18—*This charge I commit to you, son Timothy, according to the prophecies previously made concerning you, that by them you may wage the good warfare . . .*
- 1 Timothy 6:12—*Fight the good fight of faith . . .*
- 2 Timothy 2:3-4—*You therefore must endure hardship as a good soldier of Jesus Christ. No one engaged in warfare entangles himself with the affairs of this life, that he may please him who enlisted him as a soldier.*
- 2 Timothy 4:7—*I have fought the good fight, I have finished the race, I have kept the faith.*

These comments are from Paul, who, other than Jesus, is generally considered the most spirit-filled person in the New Testament. If he was so filled, why do so many passages on warfare appear? Here is the reality of his day—and ours: The greater the filling of the spirit, the more involvement in the mission of God; the more God's mission expands, the greater the warfare.

Besides Paul's writings, other New Testament writers wrote of spiritual warfare:

- James 4:7: *Therefore submit to God. Resist the devil and he will flee from you.*
- 1 Peter 5:8-9: *Be sober, be vigilant: because your adversary the devil walks about like a roaring lion, seeking whom he may devour. Resist him, steadfast in the faith, knowing that the same sufferings are experienced by your brotherhood in the world.*
- Revelation 12:7-11: *And war broke out in heaven: Michael and his angels fought with the dragon; and the dragon and his angels fought, but they did not prevail, nor was a place found for them in heaven any longer. So the great dragon was cast out, that serpent of old, called the Devil and Satan, who deceives the whole world; he was cast out with him. Then I heard a loud voice saying in heaven, "Now salvation, and strength, and the kingdom of our God, and the power of His Christ have come, for the accuser of our brethren, who accused them before our God day and night, has been cast down. And they overcame him by the blood of the Lamb and by the word of their testimony, and they did not love their lives to the death."*

All of this reflected the earlier teaching of Jesus recorded in Luke 14:31-33:

"Or what king, going to make war against another king, does not sit down first and consider whether he is able with ten thousand to meet him who comes against him with twenty thousand? Or else, while the other is still a great way off, he sends a delegation and asks for conditions of peace. So likewise, whoever of you does not forsake all that he has cannot be my disciple."

So, in what may well have been meant to be a summary statement, toward the end of his life, Paul wrote, *Finally, my brethren* . . . and proceeded to prioritize the spiritual preparation for prayer and proclamation.

TODAY'S WAR NEWS FROM THE BATTLEFIELDS

My childhood years were lived during the Korean conflict. Every Saturday morning several hundred of my friends and I would pay our nine cents and crowd into the nearby theater to watch a morning full of cartoons, cowboy movies, and to-be-continued serial thrillers. Somewhere in every Saturday morning's offerings was a feature called, "Today's News from the Battlefields." Since the news was from Korea and few of us knew where that was, we had little interest. We used this time for a bathroom or refreshment break.

While yesterday's battle news was from faraway places and seemed of little interest to 10-year olds on Saturday mornings, today's battle news is closer and of much greater interest.

Curtis Vaughan wrote, "It is a great mistake to think that in the happy hour of our conversion all trouble and strife cease. In reality, that hour marks the beginning of a lifelong warfare—not a war for our salvation, to be sure, but a war in Christian service."[1]

Like Paul we are called to be ambassadors—those who represent a King in another Kingdom. The kingdom of this world is not yet the kingdom of our God. Satan is called the *ruler of this world* (John 12:31). As we represent our God in this earthly kingdom, we encounter Satan.

While I worked on this book, I sent emails to several friends and former students presently serving in cross-cultural settings. I asked them whether in recent days they had experienced any evidences of spiritual warfare. From a missionary friend in **Mexico** I received the story of a spiritual conflict. The missionary wrote:

> We have encountered many conflicts in the spirit over the years. It does not fail when we are moving furiously in the Lord, also automatically a close friend will turn on us and speak evil or unkindly. It sets us back, but we realize that it is Satan attacking us. We get on our knees and cry out to God to protect us and help us to love this one whom Satan is using to deter the work.

From **Nigeria** we learned of a Christian educator whose home was burned in an apparent attempt to kill him. While students from another world religion claimed to be the instigators of the fire, it was clearly interpreted as an attack originating in the mind of Satan.

From **Haiti** we learned that a witch doctor was giving missionaries much trouble and hindering the advance of the gospel. Even though she sent her children to the Christian school, the witch doctor admitted that she loved her demonic powers more than she loved God.

From **Kazakhstan** we learned of another witch doctor placing demonic curses on anyone—usually a Christian—who would not give her money. Every time a Christian would get near her home, she would yell at the person to leave. After many attempts by a local pastor to share, she finally listened to the gospel, trusted, and changed Masters.

From a former student who now is a missionary in **Brazil** we learned of a demon-possessed woman who continually disrupted open-air evangelistic meetings. After intense prayer, she ceased to be disruptive. She was neither on drugs nor alcohol, nor was she mentally ill. Often she acted normal. Other times she seemed to be possessed.

From **Taiwan** we learned from a missionary who often felt that an evil spirit was in the room at night while she was attempting to sleep. She wrote, "I felt the hate and evil so much I thought I was going to die. All I could do was appeal to Jesus. Every time I did so, the evil spirit left immediately."

From a church planter in **Canada** we learned of a woman believed by many to be demon-possessed. Since she was married to a church member, she often attended church functions. Once during a Bible study she appeared in all black. After a few moments she left. The church planter said a sudden gloom seemed to be over the group. Since her presence had caused him to lose his place in this notes, he looked again at his Bible. All he saw was a blank page. After a momentary setback he called on someone else to read. As the person read, the print reappeared in his Bible.

While serving as interim pastor in a **Houston** church I personally experienced a disruption during a Sunday morning sermon. As I was concluding my sermon, two young men stood in the middle of the center section about half of the way back. Each was dressed in black. Turning their backs on each other, they walked toward the aisles on either side of their section and climbed over people as they went. When they reached the two aisles, they started toward the front of the worship center and marched in military style. Arriving at the first row simultaneously, they turned and walked toward me and then abruptly clicked the heels of their black boots and turned away. They departed the worship center through side doors. Later, as the invitation time ended and people were seated, these two young men returned to the worship center through the same side doors and repeated their steps, complete with the clicking of their heels, until they were seated again in their original seats. I discovered they were devil worshipers and had been visiting some of the youth activities. They had been observed prayer-walking (to Satan, obviously) the church facilities. Their purpose was to disrupt activities and divert the focus of those present.

Did you notice the presence of prayer and proclamation in these reports?

As reports of these incidents intensify, Ephesians 6:10-20 will help us to be better prepared for these attacks. Half of Ephesians is about grace; half is about relationships. This passage on warfare follows a teaching on the family—one of Satan's primary targets. Spiritual warfare is not about our salvation. We are not fighting to be saved or to inherit heaven. Spiritual warfare is about service and ministry, prayer and proclamation. Therefore, we must give attention to our preparation.

Earlier in this letter Paul discussed the wonderful privileges and blessings of the one who follows Jesus. He wrote about his own calling and fellowship with other believers. He wrote about relationships—husbands and wives, parents and children, servants and masters. All of these involve degrees of difficulty. If such relationships are done well, they invite serious opposition. Thus Paul closes this letter with a discussion of spiritual warfare.

AN ONGOING PERSONAL BATTLE

Before we go further, a brief personal parenthesis may be helpful. I arrive at this subject of spiritual warfare out of an experience that began at the age of 15. As an active high-school athlete and hyperactive church youth-group member, I was on my way to a church-sponsored youth activity when the car in which I rode was hit by a speeding driver who was heavily under the influence of alcohol. My neck was broken at the second vertebra. I spent the next nine months in a hospital bed engaged in among other things, learning how to pray. Little did I know that was only a prelude to later mission—and to spiritual warfare.

Out of that experience I understood God's call on my life to vocational ministry—to be on mission with a divine purpose, a purpose that would weigh heavily in the areas of prayer and proclamation. Also out of that experience was laid a foundation for understanding and withstanding later spiritual warfare.

In the midst of the 1999 shooting crisis at **Wedgwood Baptist Church in Fort Worth, TX**—my home church—I experienced an amazing revelation. I had been commissioned by the church to write a book on the shooting and its aftermath.[2] As I was interviewing other people who were present the night of the shooting, I became aware of two things:

- Many of those present described the scene as one of spiritual attack. Some used the term *spiritual warfare*. After more than 100 interviews I concluded they were correct. Whatever else happened that night, spiritual warfare was occurring.
- Many others who were present seemed to be in denial of the tragic events.

One of the counselors explained why people were having such a tough time accepting the facts. He said the human mind is like a computer. When you ask your office computer to search for a file, it hums and hums. If it finds no file, it tells you so. When we asked our minds to compute a violent shooting in our church, during which seven precious lives were taken and hundreds were traumatized, no file existed for it. So our minds just hummed and hummed and kept rejecting our request for understanding.

With this analogy I realized that my broken-neck experience at age 15 had prepared a file in my mind that would later help me understand some of the later crises I encountered. These included the shooting at our church and many other additional crises.

Allow me to describe some of the others.

On a prayer journey to the **former Soviet Union** I was on a Russian-built Aeroflot airliner that lost power at 30,000 feet in the air. While the problem was mechanical and was corrected in a matter of a few seconds, I felt as if Satan were using the experience to gently remind me that I was on his turf.

The next experience occurred on a trip to West Africa to speak on the subject of prayer at the missionary meetings in the **Gambia and Burkina Faso**. Ten days before I departed, I was at the 18th hole of the Colonial Golf Tournament in Fort Worth. Seated four rows up, I jumped off the side of the bleachers. My foot caught in the metal construction; this caused me to fall head-first to the concrete below. Extending my right hand to break the fall, I sustained a broken and dislocated right shoulder, a torn rotator cuff, and nerve damage in my right arm as well as facial cuts. I received permission to make the trip to West Africa only because my doctor had no idea what riding on African roads in a Mitsubishi pickup with no shock absorbers would be like. But I made it with my right arm in a sling. You might say that trip was made on a sling and a prayer. Did Satan cause me to fall off the bleachers? I don't know, but if not, I do know he got involved shortly thereafter.

I was on a return trip from **Senegal**, West Africa, having spoken on prayer to a group of missionaries, and became so ill I had to sit on the back seat of the airplane. I sat near the restroom for the 10-hour flight back to Texas. Need I say more? I felt as though Satan was saying, "You tried to encourage people who are working in my territory. I'll get even with you."

I took eight student-preachers to **Guatemala** to preach in evangelistic crusades as a part of the 50th anniversary of Southern Baptist work in that country. On the night before my return flight to the U.S. I became very ill. I wasn't sure I could even make the flight back. I was sick throughout the flight and the remainder of the day. I lost 11 pounds in 24 hours and was almost dehydrated. Again, I felt as though Satan was paying me back for facilitating evangelistic ministry in a place in which he was strong.

During a major prayer journey to **China, India, and the Islamic world**, toward the end of the three-week trip I developed stomach problems. Satan? Possibly.

Before the first half of a six-month sabbatical leave to **China** I was discovered to have a rare form of skin cancer—morphia basil cell carcinoma—which required four surgeries in 36 days. These were completed within days of my departure for Hong Kong. In fact, a few days before my departure, while I was leading a prayer conference in a Nashville, TN, church, a local doctor removed the final stitches from my nose. Was this Satan trying to block a ministry that not only would encourage missionaries in China but would result in a prayer-walking orientation manual that would be translated into many languages and used in many parts of the world? Probably so.

During a prayer journey to **Japan** I began to suffer from what was later diagnosed as degenerative disk problems in my lower back. Satan loves to get involved in back problems. During a prayer journey to **Macau** I experienced debilitating swelling in a joint of my left foot. Fortunately, a missionary pharmacist was able to provide me with some anti-inflammatory medication. Was Satan trying to divert my focus from ministry? I think so.

During a prayer journey to **Costa Rica** I experienced pain in my neck and left shoulder. On return to Fort Worth the problem was diagnosed as a degenerative disk problem in my neck. Satan really can be a pain in the neck!

During a prayer journey to **Hong Kong** I experienced dizzy spells in the intense heat and high humidity. Was this Satan using the weather conditions to discourage me? Maybe.

During a six-month sabbatical leave to **Germany**, on which I was teaching prayer and discipleship in a seminary, I incurred a hernia, had floaters and flashes in my right eye (initially thought to be a detached or torn retina), and observed a recurrence of what was feared to be the earlier skin cancer. Satan? Likely.

Less than two weeks before departure for **Kosovo** I injured my lower back. The next 10 days included an emergency-room visit, a doctor's-office call, a steroid shot, and various drugs. In spite of this the doctor recommended that I not make the trip because of the back-to-back flight segments of several hours' duration and the condition of the roads in Kosovo. The missionaries concurred that this was the best decision. Did Satan use a back problem to block this trip? I believe he did.

Three weeks before we were to leave on a trip to **Italy** to lead conferences on prayer and spiritual conflict, my wife was admitted to the hospital with symptoms of a heart attack. After several tests the problem was diagnosed as acid reflux, but in the process she became dehydrated and suffered an internal infection. The timing was such that we wondered whether Satan was using the episode to discourage the trip to Italy. While I cannot prove beyond a doubt that Satan was involved in any of these circumstances, I do know that while I was attempting as a faithful disciple to be on mission for God, I experienced the kinds of attacks Satan excels in—diverting attention, distorting focus, weakening witness.

In every case the ministry assignment continued, either with me or without me. The one personal cancellation was only because of doctors' orders and then only after a brief but intense argument on my part.

Charles Kettering was an inventor of the electric cash register, electric auto ignition, spark plugs, freon, leaded gasoline, safety glass, four-wheel brakes, and automatic transmission. At his death he was a holder or co-holder of more than 140 patents.

On an occasion Kettering said, "No one would ever have crossed the ocean if he could have gotten off the ship in a storm."

We must never let Satan think he can stop us in our intercessory prayer for the proclamation of the gospel, even when the storms grow intense.

What to Do When Spiritual Warfare Threatens Prayer and Proclamation

1. Acknowledge that the conflict is real and that you are personally involved in it.

2. Recognize personal battles in your life and seek to correct them.

3. Determine to never forsake your commitment to follow

God's leadership in your life regardless of Satan's attempts to influence you otherwise.

Questions for Reflection and/or Discussion

1. What evidences do you find that inform you that you or friends you know are personally involved in spiritual warfare?
2. What personal battles do you discern in your life or in the lives of friends?
3. What can you determine to do ahead of time so you will be able to stand against Satan's attacks?

[1]Curtis Vaughan, *Ephesians* in the *Bible Study Commentary*. Grand Rapids: Zondervan Publishing House, 1977, 125.
[2]Dan R. Crawford, *Night of Tragedy Dawning of Light*. Colorado Springs: Shaw Books, 2000.

Chapter 2

EMPOWERED FOR PRAYER AND PROCLAMATION

*be strong in the Lord
and in the power of His might.*

Because we are camped in enemy territory, we need to be empowered. We have lost the home-field advantage. We are strangers in a foreign land. We are players on the opponent's field. As the old spiritual said, "This world is not my home. I'm just a-passing through."

Some have pictured Christians as safe and secure inside the camp, but the camp is located in enemy territory. The watchmen on the wall dare not fail, or the camp will be under siege.

One of the more successful professional football teams revealed a few years ago that it factored into its profile of draft-eligible players a category entitled, "Playing Hurt". Its observation was that all pro-football players get hurt from time to time. The great ones play even when they are hurt. These then were the higher-rated draft possibilities. In the spiritual sense you can—and often must—play hurt when you are empowered by the proper power source.

Abraham had received a call and a promise from God. In the words of John Newton from "Amazing Grace", Abraham had gone through "many dangers, toils and snares". Even though all human odds were against God's keeping the promise, Abraham remained faithful—pressing, praying through, and playing hurt. Paul reminds us that Abraham *with respect to the promise of God . . . did not waver in unbelief but grew strong in faith, giving glory to God* (Rom. 4:20 NASB).

In service to God you sometimes have to play hurt. Oftentimes you have to serve when you are not personally strong. In times like these we need empowering. The old hymn said, "The arm of flesh will fail you, ye dare not trust your own." Martin Luther was correct in the words of his hymn, "Did we in our own strength confide, our striving would be losing."

PLUG INTO THE CORRECT POWER SOURCE CORRECTLY

Power is a common desire of all persons. We are less needful of the knowledge of a task than we are the power to accomplish it. So where is the power source and how do we plug into it correctly? It springs not from the human nature which we inherited at birth but from the divine nature breathed into us by the Holy Spirit.

Paul's words in Ephesians 6:10 will help us identify this power—*Finally, be strong in the Lord and in the strength of His might* (NASB).

The word *strong* is a strong word; it means the imparting of power into another. It is also used in Philippians 4:13—*I can do all things through Christ who strengthens me.*

Here the word *strong* is a command in the passive voice; it means to be empowered constantly with strength that originated from a source outside of self. It means to be clothed by another with a mantle of strength.

When you cut a channel from the river to the pond, the

abundant waters of the river quickly fill the pond. Likewise, when we create a channel between our lives and the power sources of God's strength, we become infused with might. What do the following items have in common: refrigerator, computer, television set, microwave oven? They all look both desirable and functional when we see them in a catalog, in a store, or online. However, they are useless apart from a power source. Likewise, our lives may offer much promise, but apart from God's power source we are virtually worthless. The armor of God described in the verses to follow, whether defensive or offensive, is worthless apart from divine power. God is the one source of inexhaustible power from which we may draw strength.

Describing Jesus with words such as *strength, power,* and *might* must have been the wildest paradox the Romans had ever heard. To the mind of the Romans the Lord of the Christians was anything but strong. He was:

- A man of gentleness
- A man that did not push himself on another, thus exhibiting greater power
- A man who turned the other cheek when smitten
- A man who, when reviled, reviled not again.

To speak of *strength* and *Lord* in the same phrase must have sounded to the Romans like speaking of a square circle. Had Paul written to his readers encouraging them to be meek in the Lord or to be patient in the Lord or to be peaceable in the Lord, the Romans would have understood. But *be strong in the Lord* was a stretch. It was because His strength sprang from a different source than their strength did. Likewise, our strength originates not from within but from an outside source. We can claim all the strength Christ has to offer us.

Any believer has cause to waver as he or she looks at the seemingly overbearing enemy standing before us. However, the believer does not stand in his or her own strength but in strength available *in the Lord.*

In recent years Linda Lee Johnson has written appropriate words:

> Be strong in the Lord, and be of good courage;
> Your mighty Defender is always the same
> Mount up with wings, as the eagle ascending;
> Vict'ry is sure when you call on His name.
>
> So put on the armor the Lord has provided;
> And place your defense in His unfailing care.
> Trust Him, for He will be with you in battle,
> Lighting your path to avoid every snare.
>
> Be strong in the Lord, and be of good courage;
> Your mighty Commander will vanquish the foe.
> Fear not the battle, for the vict'ry is always His;
> He will protect you wherever you go.
>
> Be strong, be strong, be strong in the Lord;
> And be of good courage, for He is your guide.
> Be strong, be strong, be strong in the Lord;
> And rejoice for the vict'ry is yours.₁.

Empowering is necessary because we are powerless in ourselves. Satan makes every effort to sap us of strength. However, we have a power source that if properly accessed, will offer an endless supply of divine power.

A POWERFUL PLAY ON MIGHTY WORDS

We who major on the use of words, both in our writing and in our speaking, stand in awe of Paul, who writes *in the power of His might.* It is a powerful play on mighty words; it describes the energy and its source that empowers us.

When I was young, an evangelist visited our church for a revival meeting. All week he reminded us that on Friday night he would share a personal testimony about when he was a little boy. Since this man, C. Oscar Johnson, was the largest man I had ever seen at that point in my life, I couldn't envision him ever being a little boy. So I was present on Friday night with great anticipation.

Dr. Johnson shared a childhood experience that I will never forget. He said one day some of the bullies in his school told him they were planning to beat him up. Further they planned to carry out their threat the next afternoon as he walked over the bridge on his way home from school. Oscar knew what they threatened to do, they would do.

That night Oscar was unusually quiet at the dinner table— so much so that his father pressed for what was troubling him. When Oscar explained the dilemma, the father assured him that he would be working in a field near the bridge tomorrow afternoon and would be there to meet him at the bridge and walk with him the remainder of the way to their home.

The next day the bullies took every opportunity to remind Oscar of their threat. He could barely remain silent. As he neared the bridge on his walk home, Oscar saw his father walking across the field. Taking his father's hand Oscar walked across the bridge and looked into the bushes where the bullies were hiding. Safely across the bridge, Oscar turned again toward the bullies and said, "Yah, yah, yah! Little Oscar's father is with him. You can't hurt him."

Walking safely within the empowerment of the Father—*in the power of His might*—we can turn to Satan and say, "Yah, yah, yah! My Father is with me. You can't hurt me."

Earlier in Ephesians 1:19 Paul uses *the strength of His might* to describe the power of God exerted in the raising of Jesus from the grave—*what is the surpassing greatness of His power toward us who believe. These are in accordance with the working of the strength of His might* (NASB). The former word—*strength*—is used in the New Testament only to describe supernatural power. It denotes power as an active force and means the power is exercised, as in the picture of a weight-lifter lifting weights.

The latter word—*might*—is more passive in meaning. It speaks of being strengthened, receiving strength, demonstrating power received. This picture is the same weight-lifter dressed in a tight muscle T-shirt and demonstrating that he has received power.

Both active and passive power, while equally needed in this kingdom conflict, have their source in the Father. The Spirit of God empowers us with the power of God. The same resurrection power spoken of in Ephesians 1:19 is what Paul now offers to his readers.

Biblical examples of God's strength and might are numerous.

After he had taken over the leadership from Moses, Joshua found himself in a major conflict. Standing before the fortified city of Jericho, no doubt wondering whether he could take it, Joshua saw a mighty warrior with drawn sword. Inquiring as to the man's identity the soldier said, *"As Commander of the army of the Lord I have now come"* (Josh. 5:14). God used Joshua to capture Jericho through *the power of His might*.

A major attack was being made on the Israelites by the king of Syria (2 Kings 6:11-17). Elisha was called in to give advice. There stood Elisha, God's prophet, surrounded by soldiers, chariots, and horses. Surely Syria's king must have been terrified. Elisha prophesied and prayed; God protected His people through *the power of His might*.

After the temptation experience in the wilderness Jesus was ministered to by angels (Mt. 4:11). Likewise in the Garden of Gethsemane angels sent from the Father ministered to Jesus (Luke 22:34). How did Jesus endure these experiences? He endured through *the power of His might*.

In Acts 18 Paul was having great difficulty in Corinth. Persecution had broken out. Paul was in danger for his own life. In the midst of discouragement God spoke in the night by way of a vision. Paul remained in Corinth another 18 months. How? He remained through *the power of his might*.

Finally, as Paul stood on trial for his life and no man stood with him, he prayed and concluded, *the Lord stood with me and strengthened me* (2 Tim. 4:17). How did Paul stand so strong in the face of death? He stood strong through *the power of His might*.

How often I have found myself in the midst of Satan's territory with a feeling of powerlessness. My thoughts seemed hollow. My prayers seemed empty. My words seemed futile. Then I experienced a rush of power; I almost physically experienced it—a new clarity of thought, a fresh creativity in prayer, a bold confidence in verbal expression. What caused the change? Nothing less than an infusion of spiritual power that allowed me to continue *in the power of His might*. For some reason I, who was not *strong in the Lord*, became *strong in the Lord and in the power of His might*. The whole world seemed brighter. What a difference an infusion of divine strength makes on an otherwise powerless human being!

A little girl once was asked how she faced the devil. She replied that since Jesus was in her heart, every time Satan knocked at the heart, she just asked Jesus to answer the door. She was unknowingly basing her belief on the truth expressed in Ephesians 6:10—*Be strong in the Lord and in the power of His might*. This same truth was earlier expressed in 2 Chronicles 20:15—*"Do not be afraid nor dismayed because of this great multitude, for the battle is not yours, but God's."*

STRONGHOLDS THAT DO NOT HOLD

A key Scripture related to our empowerment is 2 Corinthians 10:3-4—*For though we walk in the flesh, we do not war according to the flesh, for the weapons of our warfare are not of the flesh, but divinely powerful for the destruction of fortresses* (NASB).

When a lone gunman entered our church in the midst of a youth meeting and killed seven people before he took his own life, we had no human weapons with which to retaliate. Even though a police officer was in the building, he had no gun with him. Although a few military veterans tried to get an angle from which to rush the gunman, they could not. From a human standpoint we were defenseless. So what kept the gunman from killing dozens of people? The stained-glass window of a cross above the baptistery through which the bright evening sun was shining in blinding light may have been the reason he was diverted. Every time the gunman moved down an aisle and out from under the balcony's overhanging shadows, he was confronted with this bright cross and turned back, cursing. The actions of one 19 year-old man who stood to face the gunman and said, "Sir, you don't need to do this. You just need Jesus", may have hampered him. Within a few seconds, the gunman cursed and killed himself. *The weapons of our warfare are not of the flesh, but divinely powerful.*

The word *weapons* is plural and is used elsewhere by Paul. One example is in Ephesians 6:10-20. The translation of *The New Testament in Modern English* by J. B. Phillips may help:

> *The truth is, although of course we lead normal human lives, the battle we are fighting is on a spiritual level. The very weapons we use are not those of human warfare but powerful in God's warfare for the destruction of the enemy's strongholds. Our battle is to bring down every deceptive fantasy and every imposing defense that men erect against the true knowledge of God. We even fight to capture every thought until it acknowledges the authority of Christ.*

Because of the critical nature of these verses, some further explanation is needed. The context has Paul being accused of having a weak physical presence while he wrote bold letters. In 2 Corinthians 10:1 he addresses that accusation. He also had been accused of walking in the flesh, so he addresses that issue. Thus, when he writes 2 Corinthians 10:3-6, Paul is in the midst of responding to accusations. He admits, *we walk in the flesh* but affirms that *we do not war according to the flesh* (2 Cor. 10:3). The Greek word translated *war* (*strateuo*) is perhaps better translated *campaign,* since Paul is not referring to a military conflict but a spiritual endeavor. He is contrasting "walking in the flesh" with encountering the enemy of the flesh. He warns that when we encounter the enemy, we need supernatural weapons.

The *strongholds* (Greek, *ochuroma*) of 2 Corinthians 10:4 were fortresses. Paul used the word metaphorically to represent things in which mere human confidence is imposed. These *strongholds* could be pulled down or cast down (2 Cor.

10:5). In verse four the word *pulling down* (Greek, *kathairesis*) is used as a noun and in verse five *casting down* (Greek, *kathaireo*) is used as a verb. *Kata* means "down. *Haireo* means "take, cast, demolish." The *weapons* (Greek, *hoplon*) for accomplishing such an act (2 Cor. 10:4) are plural as used here and elsewhere when referring to spiritual warfare. Paul elaborates on these weapons in Ephesians 6:10-20. The key phrase of the passage is not *pulling down strongholds* (2 Cor. 10:4) or *casting down arguments* (2 Cor. 10:5) but *mighty in God* (2 Cor. 10:4). You cannot war with Satan in your own strength, and you certainly can't single-handedly destroy his *strongholds*. James appropriately instructs believers: *Submit to God. Resist the devil and he will flee from you* (James 4:7).

In other words victory is ours. Satan's *strongholds* do not hold. He is a defeated foe—whipped before the fight. Consider these biblical outcomes in our relationship with Satan:

- Romans 8:37—*Yet in all these things we are more than conquerors through Him who loved us.*
- Colossians 2:15—*Having disarmed principalities and powers, He made a public spectacle of them, triumphing over them in it.*
- James 4:7—*Therefore submit to God. Resist the devil and he will flee from you.*
- 1 Peter 3:22—(Jesus Christ,) *who has gone into heaven and is at the right hand of God, angels and authorities and powers having been made subject to Him.*
- Revelation 12:10-11— *"Then I heard a loud voice saying in heaven, 'Now salvation, and strength, and the kingdom of our God, and the power of His Christ have come, for the accuser of our brethren, who accused them before our God day and night, has*

been cast down. And they overcame him by the blood of the Lamb and by the word of their testimony' . . ."

While he was pastor of the Overlake Christian Church in Lakeland, WA, Bob Moorehead wrote "A Mandate to Satan":

Satan, take note and listen well! Get off my back! You will not conquer me. I'm blood-washed, Spirit-filled, daily delivered, strongly sanctified, Spirit-soaked and Word indwelt. I am linked with sovereign and eternal power and have set my face.

You're a deceiver, but you won't deceive me; you're a liar, but you won't lie to me; you're a killer, but you won't murder me; you're a roaring lion, but I'm not devourable; you're extremely subtle, but I'm on to your ways! You parade as an angel of light, but I walk in a brighter light. Your days of deception are over with me. I won't be deceived, detoured, derailed, distorted, distracted, discouraged or disillusioned by your schemes. Your vile influence won't cross the "No Trespassing" sign on the door of my heart. My life is off-limits to you now. My doors are all closed to you forever! You won't walk in, crawl in, slither in, sneak in, pry in, jump in, swim in, fly in, drive in or barge into my life. I have a permanent guest that now lives inside and HE cannot share my temple with you.

You may lure, lie, linger, lurch, laugh, lunge or leap, but you won't come in. Your days are numbered; your kingdom doomed; your designs are dwindling; your evil eroding; your devilishness dissolving; your deceit decaying; your deception diminishing and your death is dying. Your progress is poisoned, your poison is paralyzed and your penetration is profitless! Your ultimate victory has been canceled and soon your show will be over!

You can't trap me with your wares, soil me with your subtlety, or defeat me with your deception. He that is in me is greater than you! Now get off my property, for the day of your final binding is not far away! [2]

The truth is that Satan may tempt, torment, test, and try, but he cannot triumph. He would like to lift up strongholds against us, but he has no strongholds that hold up. Every time Satan shows up, God is there to offer empowerment and future victory.

The essence of empowerment is to gain both active and passive strength from the power and might of the Lord. Even though Satan will try his best to deplete your strength and short-circuit your power, he is powerless compared to the Lord. So pray in God's power for the proclamation of the gospel.

What to Do to Be Empowered
for Prayer and Proclamation

1. Be sure you are plugged into the proper power source.
2. Access spiritual strength from God's mighty power.
3. Draw strength and encouragement from biblical examples of empowerment.

Questions for Reflection and/or Discussion

1. What steps would you need to take to plug back into the proper power source? What about steps needed for friends?

2. How would you go about accessing spiritual strength from God's mighty power or suggest friends go about it?

3. Can you think of another biblical example of empowerment not mentioned in this chapter?

[1] *"Be Strong in the Lord."* Words by Linda Lee Johnson. c 1979 Hope Publishing Company, Carol Stream, IL, 60188. All rights reserved. Used by permission.

[2] Bob Moorehead, *Words Aptly Spoken.* Kirkland, WA: Overlake Christian Press, 1995, pp. 113-114.

Chapter 3

EQUIPPED FOR PRAYER AND PROCLAMATION

*Put on the whole armor of God . . .
take up the whole armor of God*

During Operation Desert Storm, I was serving as interim pastor in Lawton, OK, home of the Fort Sill Army Post. Often I would check into my motel on Saturday and then watch a Lawton television station to get updated on the local news before I put the finishing touches on my Sunday-morning sermon. Live interviews were a frequent occurrence as there were many human-interest stories among the reservists being processed through Fort Sill before they were deployed to the desert. In the course of interviewing soldiers, a television reporter asked a recently called-up reservist about his feelings on the war. His response was, "I didn't sign up to fight. I signed up for the benefits." Granted, while his represented a minority response among the many interviews conducted, his interview did not play well in a military town. Nor does such an attitude play well in spiritual arenas.

Similarly during the Operation Iraqi Freedom, one called-up reservist shared related feelings when he stated, "This is not what I had in mind when I signed up for occasional money-making weekends away from home."

The benefits of the Christian life are many, but as Satan

walks about like a roaring lion, seeking whom he may devour (1 Pet. 5:8), we must do more than count the benefits. One must equip himself or herself and prepare for conflict in the midst of prayer and preparation.

While the Christian life includes conflict and the New Testament speaks often of warfare, we are not so much warriors as ambassadors. Paul saw himself as *an ambassador in chains* and called his readers *ambassadors for Christ*. We represent our King in a kingdom in which Satan is described as *the god of this age* (2 Cor. 4:4). As we fulfill our mission of being a disciple and making other disciples, we get caught in the crossfire of the battle fought in *heavenly places*. So, Paul encouraged us to *be strong in the Lord and in the power* (active) *of His might* (passive). Having given attention to our empowering, we must now consider our equipping. Just as the strength is not from ourselves, neither is the armor from ourselves.

In Ephesians 6:11 Paul says, *Put on the whole armor of God*; in Ephesians 6:13 he tells his readers to *take up the whole armor of God*. This is the balance of the preceding statement, *be strong in the Lord . . ..* God gives us strength, but we also must do something for ourselves: *put on . . . take up*. Some have such a low self-image, they think they have nothing to contribute. Thus they fully rely on God's strength, minus equipping themselves with armor. Others have such an inflated self-image, they think they can do it all by just putting on and taking up the armor, minus God's strength.

CONFLICT AS SEEN THROUGH THE EYES OF PAUL

Since Paul's father was a Roman citizen, Paul had appealed his case to the court of the emperor, saying *"I was born a citizen"* (Acts 22:28). Thus, Paul was a prisoner of the emperor. During his time in prison he had developed a relationship with many of the elite Praetorian Guard—a group that guarded prisoners of the emperor. He wrote in Philippians 1:13, *it has become evident to the whole palace guard, and to all the rest, that my chains are in Christ.*

In other places Paul refers to being a prisoner.

- *though I have done nothing against our people, yet I was delivered as a prisoner from Jerusalem into the hands of the Romans* (Acts 28:17).
- *I rather appeal to you—being such a one as Paul, the aged, and now also a prisoner of Jesus Christ* (Philemon 9).

Beyond being a *prisoner* Paul was a prisoner *in chains.* The Greek word used here is *halusis,* which was also used in other passages:

- *"for the hope of Israel I am bound with this chain"* (Acts 28:20).
- *I am an ambassador in chains . . .* (Eph. 6:20).

The *halusis* was a short length of chain securing the wrist of the prisoner to the wrist of the guard. While it made escape nearly impossible, it nevertheless allowed for some freedom of movement.

The simple fact that Paul was *in chains* would not of itself have made any positive impact for the gospel, but the fact that his chains were *in Christ* made all the difference. Rather than being known and treated as a common criminal, guilty of some disgraceful crime, Paul became known among the guards as a prisoner for the sake of his faith. So with a prison cell for a pulpit, a few Roman guards for a congregation, and a set of chains for a clerical robe (or Sunday suit and tie), Paul proclaimed the gospel.

Can you imagine what a Roman soldier must have experienced while handcuffed to the apostle Paul for four hours? Which of the two was the real prisoner? Paul thought of himself as an *ambassador* in chains, duly commissioned to speak boldly about the Lord to whoever got near him. He was a chained *ambassador*, but he was an *ambassador* nevertheless. He wore his chains as decorations—as a badge of office and privilege.

Nor was his ultimate congregation limited to a few guards. The phrase *and to all the rest* may well refer not to other Roman guards but to the public beyond who would hear Paul's words and witness via these chained congregants. Far from closing doors, Paul's imprisonment opened new doors through which he himself might never go. Never underestimate the size of your audience. If you proclaim well, your words go far beyond your lips.

Listen to Paul's companion, Luke, share his insight into this experience: *Paul dwelt two whole years in his own rented house, and received all who came to him, preaching the kingdom of God and teaching the things which concern the Lord Jesus Christ with all confidence, no one forbidding him* (Acts. 28:30-31).

According to Roman law, a citizen could enjoy certain freedoms of personal liberty until he was brought to trial. The freedom afforded to Paul was even beyond the normal freedom offered to prisoners. Such freedom allowed Paul to write letters. Most scholars agree that from this imprisonment Paul wrote Ephesians, Colossians, Philippians, and Philemon. Not only did Paul's freedom to share with and through Roman guards advance the gospel, but the circulation of Paul's letters proved invaluable to the early church and even to this day. In addition Paul *received all who came to him* (Acts 28:30). Who visited him? We can gain insight into these visitors by looking elsewhere in the New Testament:

- Luke and Aristarchus—2 Timothy 4:11
- Timothy—Philippians 1:1; Colossians 1:1; Philemon 1
- Tychicus—Ephesians 6:21
- Epaphroditus—Philippians 4:18
- Mark—Colossians 4:10

Through Roman guards, through letters, and finally through faithful friends Paul's influence and contributions continued, even though his missionary journeys had ended. One door closed; three doors opened. God's mathematics, often misunderstood by the world, always has the correct bottom line.

For two years this continued with Paul being watched and sometimes chained to Roman soldiers, night and day. His only variety was the changing of the guard approximately every four hours. These Roman guards in their Roman armor were all dressed alike.

Have you ever noticed how similar military types look? When our son, James, graduated from Marine Boot Camp, we were in attendance. Twelve weeks earlier we had waved good-bye to him and a bunch of his new buddies as they boarded an airplane for San Diego, CA. On that day they were all shapes and sizes. But on graduation day, as the graduates marched onto the tarmac, not even mothers could identify their own sons. Everyone looked the same—like a United States Marine.

I imagine the Roman soldiers who guarded Paul all began to look alike. But Paul memorized the uniqueness and importance of each piece of their armor. He listened to their talk of battle. He applied it to the Christian life, especially the Christian's conflict with evil, and he wrote about it.

The book of Acts ends with an adverb—*akolutos,* meaning unhinderedly. This strange ending has caused some to think Acts to be incomplete. Rather, the unusual ending underscores the purpose of the book. Acts was written to record the historical expansion of Christianity through national, racial, and religious barriers without yielding to the hindrances, so the advance of the gospel would continue, beyond the historical record of Acts, *unhinderedly.*

The essence of equipping is to evaluate the circumstances, make the best of the resources, and leave the results up to God. Satan will try to make you a victim of the circumstances as well as limit your resources. God wants you to be the victor over the circumstances, just as Paul was with his circumstances. Resources for prayer and proclamation are abundant and available.

GOD'S RESOURCES AND OUR RESPONSIBILITY

God's supply is always adequate and complete. Hudson Taylor, English missionary to China for more than 50 years and the father of faith missions, said, "God's work, done God's way, will not lack God's supply." Adequate armor can only be provided by God. Inadequate armor springs from phony philosophers, amateur theologians, well-meaning televangelists, New Age grouping gurus, fatalistic futurists.

Every piece of God's resources—armor worn by a Roman soldier—is included in Paul's description except the pieces used to protect the shins from the knees to the ankles, the spear, and the small shield used in face-to-face combat. Since the soldiers Paul met were on guard duty in Rome, they would have had no need for these pieces

In *Pilgrim's Progress*, John Bunyan notes that the armor given to Christian in the House Beautiful was complete but included no protection for his back, so that in his encounters with Apollyon he could not retreat but had to stand firm and face his foe. Likewise, God provides no armor for our backs.

God has supplied the armor. Our responsibility is to pick it up and put it on—*Put on the whole armor of God* (Eph. 6:11). *Put on* is the verb tense that means you do something for yourself—in this case, arm yourself. The verb tense calls for urgent action. It is a command to act.

Take up used in verse 13 is the more common military term for arming oneself. This suggests that all of the armor needed for the conflict lies at our disposal and is provided by God. But, we must pick it up and put in on. Once the conflict begins, arming oneself will be too late.

Imagine a Roman officer giving armor to a soldier and the soldier choosing to go into battle without putting on his armor. Armor is worthless unless it is put on—as worthless as a gun in a gun rack. Only when the gun is removed does it provide worth. God's resources are as worthless as a bullet-proof vest in the trunk of the police car during a gun fight.

The sun was just coming up. The motorcycle officer moved smoothly through the quiet Los Angeles suburb on his way to work. As he neared an intersection, a red pickup truck sped past without even slowing for the stop sign. The officer turned on his flashing lights and radioed the station that he was in pursuit of the red vehicle.

As his unit pulled up behind the slowing truck, the officer was thinking, "This fellow is probably late for work." Unknown to the officer, the driver of the pickup had just robbed an all-night grocery store. On the seat beside the driver was the paper bag with the money and the gun he had used. The driver was thinking, "The cops know already." He was scared. His hand rested on the gun.

The truck pulled to the side of the road and stopped. The officer parked his motorcycle and approached the driver. He was relaxed, "Good morning sir. May I see your . . .." He didn't even finish his sentence. The driver stuck his arm out of the truck and fired his weapon. The barrel of the gun was just two inches from the officer. The bullet hit the officer in the center of his chest. He was knocked to the ground seven feet away.

For a few moments all was quiet. Then, to the horror of the gunman, the officer slowly stood to his feet. The driver couldn't believe it. "This guy must be Superman," he thought. In shock the policeman slowly began to brush the dirt from his uniform. After two or three seconds the officer regained his wits, pulled his service revolver, and fired two rounds into the side of the truck. The first round went through the open window and destroyed the windshield. The second round went through the side of the door and ripped into the driver's leg. "Don't shoot!" screamed the terrified robber as he threw the gun and the bag of money out of the window.

The officer's life had been spared because he was wearing a bullet-proof vest. Vests are incredibly strong, even though they are only about three-eights of an inch thick. They are made of dozens of layers of an extremely tough fiber called Kevlar.

A few months after the preceding incident, another officer, Ray Hicks, and his partner were attempting to serve a search warrant on a well-known drug dealer in the city of Inglewood. As his partner knocked, Hicks yelled out, "Police!" and started to kick down the door. From inside the shabby apartment four shots rang out and four slugs exploded through the door. One found its mark. The point of impact was almost exactly where the motorcycle officer had been hit just a few weeks before—squarely in the center of the chest.

Later, his partner recalled that Hicks said quietly, "I'm hit," and slowly sank to the floor. The coroner reported that Hicks probably lived less than a minute after being shot. The bullet had ruptured an artery; blood to the brain had been cut off instantly.

Police officer Ray Hicks was 27-years old. He left a wife, three children, and a bullet-proof vest in the trunk of his car, parked 30 feet from where he fell.

Every police officer in Los Angeles believes in bullet-proof vests. They work! I doubt you could find a police officer anywhere who doesn't believe vests save lives.

But that is not enough. An officer must do more than believe in vests. He must take his belief to the point of personal commitment. He must be willing to wear the vest and wear it at all times, even when the weather is hot—even when the vest is uncomfortable.[1]

In the midst of prayer and proclamation, unaware of when and where the enemy might attack, the Christian should be responsible to seek all of the armor which has been provided for him, undervaluing and omitting nothing. Once discovered, the armor must be *put on*.

So, take advantage of all of the spiritual armor God makes available for you. Satan will attempt to catch you unarmed or inadequately armed. God has provided everything you need to be properly positioned against Satan so you might intercede effectively for the proclamation of the gospel.

What to Do to Be Equipped for Prayer and Proclamation

1. Accept the challenge presented by the circumstances of your conflict with Satan.
2. Recognize God's limitless resources and take responsibility to access them.
3. With no armor provided for the back, determine to never turn your back on God, thus making yourself vulnerable to Satan.

Questions for Reflection and/or Discussion

1. What does to *put on* or *take up* the armor of God mean to you?
2. Why does Paul offer no armor for the protection of the back?
3. What would you or someone you know need to do immediately to be better equipped for prayer and proclamation?

[1]Story by: Bob Vernon, Deputy Chief (retired) Los Angeles Police Department. Reprinted from *Illustration Digest*, Winslow, AR: AA Publishing, April, 1992.

Chapter 4

POSITIONED FOR PRAYER AND PROCLAMATION

stand against . . . withstand . . . stand

Some would say that position is everything. Be in an incorrect position and all adequate preparation is weakened. Be in a correct position and even inadequate preparation can be overcome. Whatever the case, we must learn how to properly position ourselves and hold our positions.

A young soldier was describing a crucial moment in the midst of a fire fight when the smoke prevented him from seeing more than five yards in front of his gun. Discerning whether he was surrounded by the enemy or by comrades was impossible. "So, what did you do?" inquired a listener?

"What did I do?" he replied. "I just stood by my gun!"

That is our task—to stand in the place where God has assigned to us and to hold strong to our positions.

STANDING AND WITHSTANDING

We have considered Paul's view of spiritual armor as well as our responsibility to *put on* such armor. Now Paul instructs us four times to *stand* and *withstand* the enemy:

Put on the whole armor of God, that you may be able to <u>stand</u> against the wiles of the devil . . . . Therefore take up the whole armor of God, that you may be able to <u>withstand</u> in the evil day, and having done all, to <u>stand</u>. <u>Stand</u> therefore . . . (Eph. 6:11-14a).

We *stand* and *withstand* in the presence of the enemy. The Greek word for *stand* is a military term having to do with the attitude of a soldier while facing his enemy. It is a word often used in Scripture:

- Romans 5:2—Paul speaks of *this grace in which we stand.*
- 1 Corinthians 15:1—Paul refers to the gospel *in which you stand.*
- 1 Corinthians 16:13—We are challenged to *stand fast in the faith.*
- Galatians 5:1—Paul writes, *Stand fast in the liberty by which Christ has made us free . . . .*
- Philippians 1:27—We are to *stand fast in one spirit.*
- Philippians 4:1—Paul encourages us to *stand fast in the Lord.*
- Colossians 4:12—Paul wants his readers to *stand perfect and complete in all the will of God.*
- 2 Thessalonians 2:15—Paul admonishes readers to *stand fast and hold the traditions which you were taught.*

We often sing:

- "Standing on the promises . . . ."
- "Stand up, stand, up for Jesus you soldiers of the cross . . . ."
- "We are standing on holy ground . . . ."

Withstand means to successfully resist, to stand against.

The term *evil day* is not a reference to a particular day but to any day that is evil enough for Satan to attack. It is also used to refer to the day of temptation. The Psalmist proclaims, *The Lord will deliver him in time of trouble* (Ps. 41:1) and again *Why should I fear in the days of evil . . .?* (Ps. 49:5). Since the *evil day* arrives unannounced, believers are to be armed and ready with full confidence that God will deliver and protect.

In the long-buried ancient city of Pompeii guides show the remains of a Roman soldier—a rusty helmet and breastplate and a few human bones in a little stone sentry-box found by the city gate. Most people were able to flee the city before the volcano's effects arrived. Yet, some did not. Every other bit of human remains discovered in the city were found either in cellars where people hid or lying fallen on the streets under the shower of volcanic mud and ashes as people ran for their lives. So it seems this Roman soldier, with all the city's inhabitants fleeing around him and the danger of death approaching, simply stood his post and died there. We have a similar order—to stand.

In the days of the Spanish Inquisition, the tormentors found that the very worst punishment was to put a man into a cell in which the ceiling was not high enough for him to stand at full height. It broke the spirit quickly. Likewise, if we do not stand, we risk personal discouragement and ultimate failure.

RESISTING THE DEVIL

We are to *stand* resistant. Every time Jesus had a direct encounter with Satan, He quoted Scripture. He led from His strength and Satan fled.

Paul had a *thorn in the flesh* given to him *as a messenger of Satan to torment* (2 Cor. 12:7 NASB). Paul did not go on the attack against Satan. He did not rebuke him, bind him, debate him, battle him, or even speak to him. He prayed and asked God to remove the thorn. He was given sufficient grace.

Paul was hindered by Satan when trying to visit Thessalonica (1 Thess. 2:18). He did not try to break Satan's strongholds or cast him down. Rather, he focused on Jesus and on his fellow believers (1 Thess. 2:19-20).

You are not to command Satan; you are to resist him. I have been on prayer teams in which individuals issued commands to Satan. Why would you want to talk to Satan and demand that he refrain from some activity or remove himself from some place, when you have access to One infinitely more powerful and authoritative than Satan? Don't talk to Satan; talk to God about Satan. Don't look for a demon behind every bush. Look for evidence of God all around you. Don't press the enemy; praise the Victor.

James writes, *Submit therefore to God. Resist the devil and he will flee from you.* (Jas. 4:7). So how do we resist Satan?

Resist Satan by staying close to God through prayer and Bible study. Three hundred graduates of a theological seminary were surveyed. All of them admitted to some sexual sin. None of them reported having a consistent, private Bible study/prayer time. While having such is no guarantee against sin, failure to have such makes us extremely vulnerable to temptation.

Resist Satan by refuting temptation. While we cannot always control temptations, we can control our responses to them. Consider the children of Israel at the Red Sea. Some were tempted to return, some to run into the sea, some to run to mountains, but Moses said, *"Do not be afraid. Stand still, and see the salvation of the Lord, which He will accomplish for you today. For the Egyptians whom you see today, you shall see again no more forever"* (Ex. 14:13). Because they stood, they were later able to *go forward* (Ex. 14:15). Resist Satan by refusing to let him gain territory in your life. Paul wrote, *make no provision for the flesh, to fulfill its lusts* (Rom. 13:14). I often sin during mealtime. I love to visit all-you-can-eat buffets. When I do, I try to practice good stewardship. Whatever I've paid for the meal, I believe that I ought to eat twice as much to be a good steward of the financial investment. Then I go the dessert bar and sin some more. I successfully convince myself that all-you-can-eat buffets are not sinful in themselves. After all, they do include all the food groups. I doubt if the owner or manager would agree to my paying half-price and eating only half of all I can eat. The sin is my abuse.

So I have learned how to cope with the temptation of the all-you-can-eat buffet. Stay outside. I have never gained a pound at an all-you-can-eat buffet parking lot. If I make no provision for the sin of overeating, I will likely not overeat.

Resist Satan by being creative. Satan is ever-creative. We must find new ways to win the victory over temptation. If we give up and give in, we lose out—not our salvation—but certainly the joy of our salvation. Rudyard Kipling wrote:

> It was not in the open fight, we threw away the sword,
> But in the lonely watching in the darkness by the ford.

Resist Satan by learning to be content. Paul understood contentment. In Philippians 4:11-13 he wrote:

> *I have learned in whatever state I am, to be content. I know how to be abased, and I know how to abound. Everywhere and in all things I have learned both to be*

53

full and to be hungry, both to abound and to suffer need. I can do all things through Christ who strengthens me.

While the context of the passage is financial, the passage includes an application to spiritual warfare. Paul first learned something. The word *learning* originates from mystery religions and means "to be initiated . . . to learn secrets . . . to break the code." Literally the word means "I have come to learn." It speaks of entrance into a new condition.

When I was young, I was a member of the Royal Ambassador organization at our church. Because it was a missionary organization, we had a missionary password—a secret code that had to be given before we could get into the weekly chapter meetings and, more importantly to us, the football game following. Our code—DFFPSA—stood for the missionary for whom our chapter was named, Dr. Franklin Fowler, Paraguay, South America. To enter our chapter meeting by way of the secret code was to enter a new condition of learning.

While you can't always control the circumstances of your life, you can learn from them. You can learn about God. He is not so insecure that He has to explain everything to us, as we think we must do with our children. God does not owe us an explanation. God is, however, sovereign—in charge of both the circumstances and the adjustment to it.

We can also look at the state of our circumstances. The word *state* means circumstances or conditions. In 2 Corinthians 11:23-26, Paul lists a catalog of crises from his life:

• Whipped five times with 40 lashes minus one. Forty minus one was 39, the ultimate number of lashes allowed in Jewish punishment. The whip was made of several tails with sharp inserts (11:24).

- Beaten three times with rods. These beatings were applied to the spine with solid unyielding rods (11:25).
- Eight major experiences described without a complete sentence. Stoned in Lystra; shipwrecked (11:25).
- Eight different perils, all involving physical danger and hardship (11:26).
- Agonies of physical and mental exhaustion (11:27).

Paul understood difficult circumstances. His travels took him from one difficult situation to another. He was qualified to speak on the subject.

We live in a roller-coaster world. I never did like roller-coasters, even though I grew up near Playland Park in Houston (the forerunner of AstroWorld). I like the present roller-coasters even less. On a roller-coaster, you don't have time to get used to anything but change. Today, everything is changing. If some thought we were "lost in the 50s tonight," they haven't seen anything yet. At the top of their inclines, roller-coasters promise peace and tranquility. Then they tip over the top and rapid changes occur—especially to your stomach. The position at the top becomes a position on the way down—and around.

Finally, the word *content* appears only here in the New Testament. Stoics gave us this word which literally means "self-sufficient—able to withstand the shock of circumstances—not disturbed by the circumstances." *Content* describes the condition in which a person contains himself or herself and is not upset. No adequate English word for this position exists. We simply must be *content* in our prayer and proclamation.

Ultimately, we *stand* victorious. *Having done all* refers to the end of the conflict; otherwise, Paul repeats himself. When everything that can be done is done, we stand in victorious possession of the battlefield and hold the ground gained until further instructions from the Commander-in-Chief. We are not on the ground, injured, or tired. We are standing victorious when Jesus returns. Thomas Brooks said, "there are only war veterans in heaven." As victorious warriors, we stand praying and proclaiming on earth; we shall stand for eternity with Him who has already claimed the ultimate victory.

In the filming of the classic chariot-race scene in the movie, *Ben Hur*, Charlton Heston was having great difficulty staying in the chariot. He commented to director Cecil B. DeMille, "I can't stand in the chariot and win the race." DeMille replied, "It's your job to stand. It's my job to win the race." So stand, allowing God to win the race.

Finally Paul writes, *having done all, to stand*. What is this *all* to which Paul refers? Either Paul means *all* related to equipment, in other words, "having prepared all." Or it may mean *all* related to conquest—in other words, "having overcome all." Perhaps he means both. You will not only be able to stand in the midst of the conflict, but you will stand victoriously in the calm that follows.

The truth is that the race has already been won; the victory already has been claimed. Satan may do his best, but he is a defeated foe.

The Rev. Dudley Tyng gave his final message to the Philadelphia YMCA Noon Prayer Meeting during the Prayer Revival of 1858, then was killed in a farm-related accident that same week. The following Sunday, the hymnwriter, George Duffield, Jr., preached on Eph. 6:14 and wrote these verses as his conclusion:

Stand up, stand up for Jesus, ye soldiers of the cross;
Lift high his royal banner, it must not suffer loss:

From vict'ry unto vict'ry His army shall he lead,
Till ev'ry foe is vanquished, and Christ is Lord indeed.
Stand up, stand up for Jesus, the trumpet call obey;
Forth to the mighty conflict, in this His glorious day:
Ye who are men now serve Him against unnumbered foes;
Let courage rise with danger, and strength to strength oppose.

Stand up, stand up for Jesus, stand in His strength alone;
The arm of flesh will fail you, ye dare not trust your own:
Put on the gospel armor, each piece put on with pray'r;
Where duty calls, or danger, be never wanting there.

Stand up, stand up for Jesus, the strife will not be long;
This day the noise of battle, the next the victor's song:
To him who overcometh a crown of life shall be;
He, with the King of glory, shall reign eternally.

So, stand while:
- the fearful are running away
- the casual are just standing around
- the lazy are reclining on beds of ease
- the stubborn are sitting on their hands
- the defeated are slouched in defeat
- the depressed are drooped in despair
- the apathetic are disinterested in it all

Stand because:
- You are made in the image of God
- You've been redeemed by the Son of God
- You've been empowered by the spirit of God
- You're a child of the King
- You're called to a higher calling
- Your reservation in heaven is secure

Stand tall, proud, prepared, privileged, victorious.

So, stand resistant and victorious against Satan. All of his methods and strategies will ultimately fail as we faithfully stand and withstand in our intercessory prayer for the proclamation of the gospel.

What to Do to Be Positioned for Prayer and Proclamation

1. Stand and withstand all of Satan's onslaughts against you.
2. Allow God to win the battle while you faithfully stand your ground.
3. Understand that the victory is assured even though the battle still rages.

Questions for Reflection and/or Discussion

1. What does to *stand* and *withstand* against Satan mean for you?
2. Identify the ground on which you or a friend presently stand and explain how you, or that person, can stand *content*.
3. What role does your position have in prayer and proclamation?

Chapter 5

STRATEGIES AGAINST PRAYER AND PROCLAMATION

the wiles of the devil

Strategies are crucial in warfare; Satan has an abundance of them. Paul supplies us with no resume of Satan, nor does he busy himself with a discussion of Satan's origin. He assumes Satan's existence and trusts his readers do as well. His purpose is not to define or describe Satan but to warn the readers of the strategies—*the wiles of the devil*—that will be used against them.

AISLES OF FILES OF WILES

I once had a colleague who saved everything. His wastebasket was always empty. In the days before computer files this colleague saved thousands of pages of paper in metal file cabinets that lined his office. We affectionately named his office, "Aisle of Files." With Satan's multitude of strategies—*wiles*—this section of the book might be called, "Aisles of Files of Wiles."

As we represent Jesus Christ in our lives and by our witness, we will undergo satanic attack. Temptations, diversions, and distortions will surround us. *The wiles of the devil* (Eph. 6:11) refers to the many, many methods of Satan—aisles and aisles of them. Against all of his methods, strategies, and plans, we must stand and never turn our backs.

The Greek word for *wiles* means a deliberate plan or system and is translated earlier in Ephesians 4:14 as *craftiness*. The construction of the sentence is that of an infinitive expressing purpose. With purpose the Christian is to arm himself of herself against the *wiles* of the devil. Various translations of Ephesians 6:11 translate the word *wiles* as:

- *schemes*—New American Standard Bible; New International Version
- *tactics*—Holman Christian Standard Bible
- *devices*—New English Bible
- *methods*—The New Testament in Modern English, J.B. Phillips
- *evil tricks*—Good News Bible

Whatever *wiles* is called, we know that Satan not only plans his attacks but capitalizes on circumstances caused by others. This creates significant conflict.

Internal *wiles* will occur. The contrast between what we do and what we desire to do is obvious even at an early stage of spiritual development. Our intentions are good. Our actions often do not match.

Paul understood this internal conflict. *For the good that I will to do, I do not do; but the evil I will not to do, that I practice* (Rom. 7:19).

One of the ways Satan tries to break through our armor is temptation. Temptation is normal. We are made with both needs and desires. If we didn't need to eat, some of us would starve, but that's no excuse for overeating. If we didn't need sleep, some would stay up all night, but that's no excuse for laziness. If you are never tempted, don't brag about it; see a physician.

Some have destroyed marriages for a few minutes of yielding to temptation. Others have destroyed relationships by a yielding to untruth or acting with a lack of integrity. Still others have destroyed their bodies by yielding to the temptation to put the wrong things into their bodies or failing to take care of the body.

In all of these internal conflicts Satan has plans—*wiles*—to get the best of us.

External *wiles* also will occur. An overabundance of evil exists in the world. This affects us daily. The eradication of this evil motivates missionary activity, evangelism strategies, church-starting efforts, and benevolent programs, but evil cannot be eliminated until Jesus returns. We can only stand against it and believe that God is at work behind the scenes, but in so doing we are affected by it.

When the cancer on my nose seemed to threaten my six-month sabbatical leave to China, God said to go. Satan said not to go. Because I listened to God, a prayerwalking guide was developed that now has been translated into many, many languages—all for the glory of God. God won. Satan lost. Nonbelievers were confused. Why would I not just stay at home and rest and heal? Life is always that way. Faith always looks foolish to those who have none.

The world chuckled over the crucifixion of Jesus, while God was turning that middle cross into a throne of glory and its occupant into the Judge of this world.

The world shouts with glee as flames consume another Christian or lions tear apart another bold believer. This was the case in 197 A.D. during Roman persecution of Christians. So devastating was this persecution that Tertullian, an early church leader born in North Africa, wrote a letter to the Roman governor and refuted false charges being made against Christians and the Christian faith. He argued that Christians were in fact loyal subjects of the empire.

The writings of Quintus Septimius Florens Tertullianus, commonly known as Tertullian, were published in a volume entitled *The Apology.* From this work arose the often-used misquote, "the blood of the martyrs is the seed of the Church."

While true, the actual quote was, "the oftener we are mown down by you, the more in number we grow; the blood of Christians is seed."

Indeed, the *wiles of the devil* has continually produced more believers, more churches, more missionary endeavors, and more advance of the gospel than could possibly have been predicted by casual observers.

Yet, Satan still works through his *wiles.* We must be equipped with spiritual armor to *stand* against them.

William Gurnall, a 17th-century Puritan, wrote what may be the lengthiest book on spiritual warfare entitled *The Christian in Complete Armor: A Treatise of the Saint's War Against the Devil.* In his book he identifies six times in which Satan attacks believers.

1. When the Christian is newly converted.
2. When the Christian is afflicted.
3. When the Christian has achieved some notable success.
4. When the Christian is idle.
5. When the Christian is isolated from others who share his or her faith.
6. When the Christian is dying.[1]

So we position ourselves against the *wiles of the devil.* We resist him, even though his strategies are clever and crafty. He will scheme and plot to discourage and divert you from your desire to be a faithful disciple and maker of disciples, but he is a loser.

THE DEVIL MADE ME DO IT, BUT HOW?

Several years ago, a popular TV comedian used the famous line, "The devil made me do it." The line was always used as an excuse for being caught in some activity that was unacceptable, illegal, or undesirable. Indeed the devil does make us do some things. Now that we have some insight into who Satan is, we must consider how he persuades us to do what he wants us to do or how he hinders us from doing what we ought to do.

A good example of Satan's hindering power is found in 1 Thessalonians 2:17-20. Paul longed to visit the believers in Thessalonica. He reminded his readers that he had been *taken away from you for a short time*. His love for them was expressed in a question-and-answer format—*For what is our hope, or joy, or even crown of rejoicing? Is it not even you . . .?* However, Paul's visit to Thessalonica was not to be—*Satan hindered us*.

How does Satan hinder us? How does the devil make us do it? In his wonderful little book *Fruitful Discipleship*, Edward Thiele wrote that the satanic conflict in the New Testament was characterized by various military strategies, some of which are still in use today.[2]

Frontal assault. We are all vulnerable in some places. James writes, *But each one is tempted when he is drawn away by his own desires and enticed* (Jas. 1:14). Satan knows these places. He tempted Adam and Eve through an attractive proposition offered in opposition to God's command. Satan's temptations to Jesus were similar—turn stones to bread for food after 40 days of fasting; jump off the temple, and angels will attend to you to fulfill Scripture; worship Satan and kingdoms which you came to claim will be yours.

Siege or blockade. When we become isolated from other Christians, Satan attempts to encircle us and cut us off further from the strength gained from fellowship. Young people away at college or in the military or on a job are particularly susceptible to this strategy, as are young couples living away from home for the first time. Removed from our support systems, Satan can more easily have his way with us. He is a *roaring lion*. Remember that lions only attack the ones who wander away from the group. They prowl around and seek whom they might devour.

Ambush. Satan likes to attack when we least expect it—a sneak attack. In spiritual matters we least expect Satan to attack when we are on the crest of a successful spiritual wave—proud and relaxed, preoccupied with personal prestige.

Invasion or occupation. This is Satan's attack-and-control method. He uses addictions that did not seem so serious on initial temptation. Demon-possession was an early form of this method. Today we can be possessed with many "demons."

Infiltration. Satan likes to work through people close to us—those whom we perceive to be on our side. Satan influenced Peter to try to steer Jesus from going to Jerusalem when Jesus said He must go there to die.

Likewise, satanic conflict in the New Testament was characterized by satanic deception. Satan is the master of lies. Here are some of his lies, with Scripture rebuttal.

God is not good. *And we know that all things work together for good to those who love God, to those who are the called according to His purpose* (Rom. 8:28).

Your body is your own. *Or do you not know that your*

body is the temple of the Holy Spirit who is in you, whom you have from God, and you are not your own? For you were bought with a price; therefore glorify God in your body and in your spirit, which are God's (1 Cor. 6:19-20).

Sinful living is beneficial. *For the wages of sin is death, but the gift of God is eternal life in Christ Jesus our Lord* (Rom. 6:23).

God will forsake you. *"I will never leave you nor forsake you"* (Heb. 13:5).

This life is all you have. *"Do not lay up for yourselves treasures on earth, where moth and rust destroy and where thieves break in and steal; but lay up for yourselves treasures in heaven, where neither moth or rust destroys and where thieves do not break in and steal. For where your treasure is, there your heart will be also"* (Mt. 6:19-21).

You are what you make of yourself. *For we are His workmanship, created in Christ Jesus for good works, which God prepared beforehand that we should walk in them* (Eph. 2:10).

God doesn't love you. *"For God so loved the world that He gave His only begotten Son, that whoever believes in Him should not perish but have everlasting life"* (John 3:16).

Evil is to be feared. *God has not given us a spirit of fear, but of power and of love and of a sound mind* (2 Tim. 1:7).

God doesn't keep His promises. *The Lord is not slack concerning His promise, as some count slackness, but is longsuffering toward us, not willing that any should perish* (2 Pet. 3:9).

We have many paths to God. *Jesus said, "I am the way, the truth and the life. No one comes to the Father except through Me"* (John 14:6). *Nor is there salvation in any other, for there is no other name under heaven given among men by which we must be saved* (Acts 4:12).

90-MILES-AN-HOUR DOWN A DEAD-END ROAD

A Country music song spoke of life in a small town and the desire to escape. Since no real way to escape seemed to exist, the refrain of the song was "90-miles-an-hour down a dead-end road." This is a good description of Satan. He is a born (or should we say created?) loser. He cannot and will not win. Try as he might, he is headed down a dead-end road, complete with all his *wiles*.

Perhaps the best-known illustration of Satan as a loser is found in the Old Testament description of the life of Job, who truly was one of history's most remarkable men. Job suffered bitter physical, mental, and spiritual anguish and often did this without a sense of God's presence. In the struggle to understand life, Job began to understand both the sovereignty of God and the limitations of Satan.

While he is a formidable enemy, Satan has limitations. Satan could not touch Job. Even though Job lost much—almost everything—*And the Lord said to Satan, "Behold, all that he has is in your power, only do not lay a hand on his person"* (Job 1:12).

Satan is limited in <u>authority</u>. Only God is sovereign. This is evident in Satan's relationship with Peter, when Jesus said, *"Simon, Simon! Indeed, Satan has asked for you, that he may sift you as wheat. But I have prayed for you, that your faith should not fail"* (Luke 22:31-32).

Satan is limited in <u>knowledge</u>. Only God has all-knowledge. Satan may know more than you, but he never knows more than God.

Satan is limited in <u>power</u>. Only God has all-power. Satan has great power, but not more than God. *"Do not fear, for those who are with us are more than those who are with them"* (2 Kings 6:16). *He who is in you is greater than he who is in the world* (1 John 4:4).

Finally, Satan is limited in <u>presence</u>. Only God is omnipresent. Satan cannot be everywhere at once. He can only be in one place at a time. Thus he has to depend on his demons and angels. They have even less authority, knowledge, and power than Satan himself does.

As Satan tempted Job, he was so limited that it was like going 90-miles-an-hour down a dead-end road.

If Job is the best-known illustration of Satan's limitations in the Old Testament, the New Testament's best illustration is Satan's encounter with Jesus before His public ministry began. In Luke 4:1-13 we have three rather intense temptations that originate from Satan and are directed at Jesus.

Immediately after His baptism, Jesus went to the wilderness for a 40-day season of prayer and fasting in preparation for this public ministry. After that spiritual experience Jesus was approached by Satan. The writer of Hebrews states that Jesus was *in all points tempted as we are, yet without sin* (Heb. 4:15). Here Jesus was tempted in three *points* of life— physical, material, and spiritual—three *wiles of the devil.*

The first temptation was one of a physical nature— *"command this stone to become bread"* (Luke 4:3). One might think that after 40 days of fasting Jesus would be hungry—and that Satan was tempting Jesus at a point of weakness. However, it actually may have been at a point of strength. After all, if you have fasted for 40 days, surely one more day is possible. Nevertheless, Jesus resisted the temptation with an Old Testament quote—*"Man shall not live by bread alone, but by every word of God"* (Luke 4:4; Deut. 8:3).

Taking Jesus up on a high mountain peak Satan offered the second temptation, which was of a material nature: *"All this authority I will give You, and their glory . . . if you will worship before me, all will be Yours."* Often what Satan offers is not really his to offer. Nevertheless, Jesus again resisted and quoted an Old Testament verse— *"You shall worship the Lord your God, and Him only you shall serve"* (Luke 4:8; Deut. 6:13).

Finally, Satan took Jesus to a high pinnacle of the Temple in Jerusalem and offered a temptation that was spiritual in nature— *"If You are the Son of God, throw Yourself down from here"* (Luke 4:9). This challenge was followed by a quotation of Scripture from Satan— *"For it is written, 'He shall give His angels charge over you, To keep you,' and 'In their hands they shall bear you up, lest you dash your foot against a stone'"* (Luke 4:10-11; Ps. 91:11-12). Proving that Satan is a poor Swordsman compared to Jesus, the Lord once again resisted temptation with an Old Testament quote— *"You shall not tempt the Lord your God"* (Luke 4:12; Deut. 6:16).

All three temptations required compromise. Even to this day that is one of Satan's most effective *wiles*. If he can get us to compromise, we are weakened in our faith, those around us are disappointed in the integrity of our witness, and God is not glorified. So how shall we resist? Jesus offers a big clue: memorize, apply, and quote Scripture. The Bible is, after all, the Sword of the Spirit—our only offensive weapon in the battle with Satan.

When the resistance was over and Jesus was once again victorious over Satan, the Scripture says, *the devil . . . departed from Him until an opportune time* (Luke 4:13). One skirmish does not make a war. One triumph over Satan does not signal total victory. The temptations continue. Likewise so must the resistance.

Both the story of Job and the story of Jesus are reminders of yielding not to temptation. The following hymn text is old (1897) and has long since disappeared from many modern hymnbooks, not to mention overhead transparencies and

Power Point images.

> Yield not to temptation, for yielding is sin;
> Each vic-t'ry will help you some other to win;
> Fight manfully onward, dark passions subdue,
> Look ever to Jesus, He'll carry you through.

Temptation is not sin. In fact temptation is absolutely normal. Yielding to temptation is the sin. Neither Job nor Jesus yielded to the temptations of Satan.

Even though he has limitations and temptations, Satan does have frustrations. What good is accomplished by racing 90-miles-an-hour if the road is a dead end? How frustrating for Satan to keep going down dead-end roads. For every 90-miles-an-hour ride offered by Satan, God reveals a dead end—and offers a detour onto a "Highway of Holiness" (Isa. 35:8). Awaiting Satan is one major, final roadblock. When his limits are all reached, his temptations all spent, and his racing days are over, his *wiles* will be worthless.

Being able to identify the enemy and his *wiles* is not enough. You must also know about the enemy. Why do military leaders develop war plans based on who the enemy is? Why do coaches develop game plans depending on who the opponent is? Because the offense will be more effective once we understand the defense of the enemy/opponent. Satan does not want you to know about him. God desires that we understand our enemy. So do you endure the warfare aware or unaware? That is the question. For every aware or unaware question God offers an answer—His very presence. So continue to intercede to the Father for the proclamation of the gospel.

What to Do to Be Prepared
with Strategies for Prayer and Proclamation

1. Identify the *wiles of the devil* and resist them.
2. Identify which of the five military strategies Satan has used on you or on a friend.
3. Identify which of the satanic lies mentioned in this chapter Satan has used on you or a friend.

Questions for Reflection and/or Discussion

1. What are some internal *wiles* or strategies that Satan has used on you or a friend
2. What are some external *wiles* or strategies that Satan has used on you or a friend?
3. Besides the lies mentioned in this chapter, what other lies has Satan used on you?

---

[1]William Gurnall, *The Christian in Complete Armor: A Treatise of the Saint's War Against the Devil.* (1662-65; reprint, Carlisle, PA: Banner of Truth Trust, 1979, p. 74.

[2]W. Edward Thiele. *Fruitful Discipleship: A Guide to Personal Spiritual Growth.* New Orleans: Insight Press, 1994, pp. 148-49.

Chapter 6

OPPOSED IN PRAYER
AND PROCLAMATION

principalities ... powers ...
rulers of the darkness ...
spiritual hosts of wickedness

I had taken the group of 10 seminary students on a prayer
journey to a West African nation, but what they encountered
was not covered in our orientation notes. One day, as they
were visiting with one of the missionaries in a small church
building, a woman entered and asked for assistance. As she
explained her situation, she began to moan and groan and then
fell to the floor, writhing uncontrollably. The missionary
explained to the students that the woman had just encountered
a satanic attack and requested their assistance. For almost two
hours, the students and the missionary physically held the
woman and prayed to God that she would be set free of whatever demonic spirit had affected her. Finally, the woman's
body went limp. Within a few moments she began to praise
God and thank the students.

While this kind of situation is very difficult for Western
Christians to believe, such stories from the "mission field" are
legion. Every cross-cultural missionary I know—and I know
hundreds—has at least one story similar to this one. The closer
believers get to the front lines of the battle with Satan, the

more intense the conflict seems to become. However, sometimes the front lines are at your own front door.

Paul suggests an army of Satan's warriors is ready to attack: *principalities . . . powers . . . rulers of the darkness . . . spiritual hosts of wickedness*. According to Isaiah 14:12-15, Satan's origin was one of a fallen angel, *Lucifer, son of the morning*, cast out of heaven because of his attempts to overthrow God's throne. Depending on your view of Revelation, John seems to indicate that as many as one-third of the angels in heaven were thrown out with Satan.

Sometimes when we fall under Satan's attack, we are *struck down* or *cast down*. The language used by Paul in 2 Corinthians 4:9 is clearly that of conflict. The verb *katabakkein,* translated into the English words *struck down*, can mean laid low by a blow or a weapon. But, as Paul exclaims, we are never *destroyed*. We may be badly beaten, but we are never defeated. We may lose an occasional skirmish, but we never lose the contest. We may be knocked down, but we are never knocked out. While occasional stress fractures may occur in our earthly vessels, we are forever held together by the power of divine adhesive.

To think about Satan and the direct conflict that he brings into our lives is an awesome experience. We dare not tread too lightly nor too intensely here. We must seek a balance. C. S. Lewis made one of the most often-quoted statements related to Satan: "There are two equal and opposite errors into which our race can fall about the devils. One is to disbelieve in their existence. The other is to believe, and to feel an excessive and unhealthy interest in them. They themselves are equally pleased by both errors . . . ."[1.]

So who is the enemy, described in this four-fold terminology?

WE HAVE MET THE ENEMY
AND HE LOOKS HARMLESS

We are not sure how long Adam and Eve lived in a perfect garden-world before they met Satan. He appears first in Genesis 3:1. Before that, perfect peace and pleasant harmony existed in the garden. Then came deception and temptation, chaos and disorder. While the record in Genesis 3 leaves many blanks to be filled in, some of these are completed by passages on Satan in Isaiah 14:12-15 (*you are fallen from heaven*) and Ezekiel 28:12-19 (*You were perfect in your ways from the day you were created, Till iniquity was found in you*). To believe Scripture is to believe in a personal devil. The author of *The Exorcist,* William Friedkin, reportedly said, "It may be difficult to believe in God in this century, but one would be a fool not to believe in a personal devil."

The first reference in the Bible to evil tells us that Satan is a *serpent* (Gen. 3:1). In the history of religions, beginning in Genesis 3, the serpent is always a sinister animal.

The scene here was a perfect garden, indwelt by perfect creations of a perfect God. Like everything else, the *serpent* had been created by God. He had been given a name like all other creatures (Gen. 2:19). Not content to live outside the garden, this serpent had crept in. The fact that the *serpent* had the ability to speak indicates that he was more than just a snake. As yet the first sin had not been committed. This was still a perfect world. However, as a result of the temptations offered to the woman by the serpent—and the yielding to that temptation—sin entered the garden.

In the remaining verses of Genesis 3, we learn the sphere of Satan's activities, the method of his approach, the form of his temptations, and the certainty of his eventual overthrow and destruction.

The first thing the Bible tells us about the *serpent* is that Satan is *more cunning than any* (Gen. 3:1). Consider the stages of the temptation.

The serpent stirred the woman's curiosity by speaking to her. Surely the woman had not seen anything like this before. She had to be stunned and intrigued by a snake that talked.

The serpent then raised suspicion about God by asking, *"Has God indeed said, 'You shall not eat of every tree of the garden'?"*. This question is designed to make one think, to re-evaluate, to reconsider that which had heretofore been assumed. Initially it creates doubt. That was Satan's subtle plan.

The serpent expands his use of doubt of God to his approach. He raised three points of consideration:

- How can God be good if He places restrictions on you (Gen. 3:1)?
- God knows you will not die if you eat the fruit but rather know *"good and evil"* (Gen. 3:5).
- Actually, rather than dying, you *"will be like God"* if you eat this fruit (Gen. 3:5).

Finally, the serpent leads the woman to unbelief and eventually to disobedience. Satan's words created the appearance to the woman that the serpent knew God better than she did. This caused her to step out of the circle of trust and obedience into the circle of distrust and disobedience. Every time since then, when people believe they or Satan knows more than God, conflict has followed.

The entire temptation was based on creating in the woman a disbelief of the words of God. This still happens today. Satan would love to have you disbelieve all or parts of God's Word—the Bible.

In addition to being called a *serpent* and being described as *cunning*, Satan was and is able to communicate with human beings.

We should not be so concerned with what the serpent was as what it said. Obviously serpents don't talk, but this was much more than your average garden snake. How do we know the voice of the serpent in the garden was actually the voice of the devil himself? Consider the following passages of Scripture:

- John 8:44: *"You are of your father the devil . . . . He was a murderer from the beginning, and does not stand in the truth, because there is no truth in him. When he speaks a lie, he speaks from his own resources, for he is a liar and the father of it."*
- 2 Corinthians 11:3: *But I fear lest somehow, as the serpent deceived Eve by his craftiness, so your minds may be corrupted . . ..*
- 1 Timothy 2:14: *And Adam was not deceived, but the woman being deceived, fell into transgression.*
- Revelation 12:9: *So the great dragon was cast out, that serpent of old, called the Devil and Satan, who deceived the whole world . . ..*
- Revelation 20:2: *He laid hold of the Dragon, that serpent of old, who is the Devil and Satan.*

And still the devil is deceitful and cunning, disguising himself in various ways. You can take the devil out of your theology as some have done. You can remove his name from your hymnbook as some have done. You can banish him from society as some have done. He just keeps on with his destructive work.

In conflict an unforgivable and to some extent an uncorrectable mistake is to underestimate the enemy. Similar to the popular Energizer Bunny of television commercial fame, Satan takes a licking, but he keeps on ticking. Actually, he just keeps on talking. The communication never stops. The classic image of a little devil on one shoulder and a little angel on the other, both trying to persuade you to do it their way, is not far from the truth.

Contrary to popular opinion Satan is not simply the "old devil", as we sometimes refer to him. This depicts an aged, fragile, senile, ready-for-the-old-folks-home image. While he is old in the sense of how long he has been on the earth, he is also young, new, creative, attractive, and vivacious.

Back to Genesis 3. When the devil has done his work, he departs, slithers off into the shadows, and leaves the woman alone to contemplate. Finally she decides that the serpent was correct; she yields to the temptation offered. Then the tempted became the temptress and leads her husband into the same dreadful disobedience.

Why do we spend so much time defining and discussing Satan? John R.W. Stott answers this way:

A thorough knowledge of the enemy and a healthy respect for his prowess are a necessary preliminary to victory in war. Similarly, if we underestimate our spiritual enemy, we shall see no need for God's armor, we shall go out to do battle unarmed, with no weapons but our own puny strength, and we shall be quickly and ignominiously defeated.[2]

The opposition is related to the unchanging aspect of Satan. He has thousands of years of experience at what he does. When his experience encounters your inexperience, conflict occurs. However, be not alarmed. Even though Satan has vast experience, God has even more. For every satanic conflict that travels your way, God stands ready to strengthen you.

BIBLICAL DESCRIPTIONS OF THE ENEMY

Throughout the Bible are numerous names and descriptions for the enemy. Some of these are:

* *Satan*—adversary/opposer—is the most common name for the enemy. The name is used 56 times in Scripture. For instance Paul said in 1 Thessalonians 2:18, *Satan hindered us.*
* *Devil*—slanderer/accuser—is used 35 times in the New Testament. For instance Peter referred to *your adversary the devil* in 1 Peter 5:8.
* *Beelzebub* is used seven times.
* Jesus called Satan *"the ruler of this world"* in John 12:31.
* *The prince of the power of the air* was Paul's description in Ephesians 2:2.
* *Deceiver* is used in 2 Corinthians 11:3.
* *The tempter* is the description used in 1 Thessalonians 3:5.
* *The god of this age* is a term used in 2 Corinthians 4:4.
* *A roaring lion* is a description in 1 Peter 5:8.
* *The accuser of our brethren* is a title in Revelation 12:10.
* *Beast* is used in Revelation 19:19.

One of the clearest and most descriptive references to Satan occurs as Paul describes the enemy this way: *For we do not wrestle against flesh and blood, but against principalities, against powers, against the rulers of the darkness of this age, against spiritual hosts of wickedness in the heavenly places* (Eph. 6:12). We need to explore this verse in more detail.

Paul begins by describing the intensity of our involvement with Satan by using the word *wrestle*. The word literally means "to throw" or "to swing." From this image is derived the picture of throwing or swinging an opponent to the ground. The word is both an athletic word and a military term. In the military sense it portrays two enemies in hand-to-hand combat. They stand face to face until one of them falls.

In the idea of wrestling, we have a keynote of our faith. Wrestling is a strong word. Emotion has a place. True belief is a necessity. But without a stern struggle with evil, mixed with a strong laying hold of the good, our faith is less than deserving of its name.

From Taiwan arrive stories of the "bed ghost." Many Taiwanese experience these visitations from Satan in the night. One missionary shared that the presence was so strong that she felt heat radiating to her body from an evil presence in the room. On another occasion she felt pushed down on her bed; she felt as though she almost was suffocating. In these and similar instances, Paul's ancient word *wrestle* takes on modern significance.

Sometimes we are deceived to the point of wrestling with the wrong enemy—*flesh and blood*. So often we fight against people who may be associated with evil. They are but the visible instruments of the evil one. How much energy do we waste fighting the wrong enemies? They are not the source of evil but instead the means by which the evil one does his work.

A likely order of demonic hierarchy exists. The word *principality* and the word *powers* occur together in Ephesians 1:21 and Colossians 2:10; the words *principalities* and *powers* appear together in Colossians 1:16 and 2:15, so they are probably meant to be together here. Knowing exactly to what this refs, except to the power of Satan, is difficult. Principalities may refer to the rank and rule of demonic forces. *Powers* may allude to the power allowed them.

All of these entities owe their very existence to Christ. *For by Him were all things created that are in heaven and that are on earth, visible and invisible, whether thrones or dominions or principalities or powers. All things were created through Him and for Him* (Col. 1:16, underline mine). Jesus is *the head of all principality and power* (Col. 2:10, underline mine).

Paul further describes the enemy with the phrase *rulers of the darkness of this age* (Eph. 6:12). This world is filled with darkness. Paul may be referring back to 2 Corinthians 4:4, where he wrote of those who are perishing: . . . *the god of this age has blinded, who do not believe, lest the light of the gospel of the glory of Christ, who is the image of God, should shine on them* .

Then a further description of Satanic forces follows—*spiritual hosts of wickedness in the heavenly places* (Eph. 6:12). This may be a summary of the entire list of demonic creatures, rather than a new category.

Some see all of these as people in high places of government such as rulers who were persecuting the church. But this negates Paul's own words, that the real enemy is not *flesh and blood*. People are instruments of the enemy, but they are not the enemy. It is difficult to conclude anything other than that the Jesus portrayed in the gospels believed in demons. In fact, exorcism was an integral part of His ministry. If Jesus believed in the demonic and spoke of the demonic, we would be well served to accept these categories as features of the demonic.

Nor do these passages describe several classes of demons; they include several descriptions of the same enemy. Satan is multi-talented.

Once a boxer was getting beat up in the ring. After each

round he staggered to his corner. His trainer would say to him, "He's never touched you yet." Several rounds of cuts, bruises, and bleedings later and on hearing the same words from his trainer, the boxer exclaimed, "Keep an eye on the referee, 'cause someone in this ring is beating the stuffing out of me." Satan can hit us from many directions and in many forms.

High places or *heavenly places* refers to the battlefield. The phrase is used five times in Ephesians. It is not a reference to a geographical location but to a supernatural one.

Modern warfare has coined a new phrase—*surgical bombing of targets of opportunity*. It refers to a long-distance attack from either an aircraft or a missile-launching ship. While Satan does on occasion create this type of long-range conflict, the reference here is to hand-to-hand combat.

Remember this conflict is God versus Satan, not you or me versus Satan. We are simply caught up in the crossfire. Thus the real battlefield is in invisible regions of the spirit world. Any conflict is made more difficult when the enemy is veiled. Identify the enemy, and then *Resist the devil* (Jas. 4:7) as you faithfully intercede for the proclamation of the gospel.

How to Meet the Opposition with Prayer and Proclamation

1. Ask God what lessons you should be learning in the midst of the conflict.

2. Ask God to assist you in not yielding to the temptations of Satan.

3. Claim victory over the conflict even as you are in the process of coping with it.

Questions for Reflection and/or Discussion

1. In what form has Satan appeared to you or to a friend of yours?
2. How would you describe Satan?
3. Can you identify specific resources God is making available to you or to a friend?

[1]C. S. Lewis. *The Screwtape Letters*. New York: The MacMillan Company, 1959, p. 9.

[2]John R.W. Stott, *The Message of Ephesians*. Downers Grove, IL: InterVarsity Press, 1979, p. 263.

Chapter 7

ARMED FOR PRAYER AND PROCLAMATION

*Stand therefore, having girded your waist
with truth, having put on the breastplate
of righteousness, and having shod your feet
with the preparation of the gospel of peace*

We have been empowered for encounters with the enemy, equipped with the *whole armor of God*, positioned for the conflict, and informed of the enemy and his strategies. We now must consider the specific pieces of spiritual armor.

The Bible often speaks of equipping:

- Isaiah 11:4-5: *with righteousness He shall judge the poor, And decide with equity for the meek of the earth; He shall strike the earth with the rod of his mouth, And with the breath of His lips He shall slay the wicked. Righteousness shall be the belt of His loins, And faithfulness the belt of His waist.*
- Isaiah 59:17: *For He put on righteousness as a breastplate, and a helmet of salvation on His head; He put on the garments of vengeance for clothing, And was clad with zeal as a cloak.*
- 2 Corinthians 6:7: *by the word of truth, by the power of God, by the armor of righteousness on the right hand*

and on the left . . ..
- 1 Thessalonians 5:8: *But let us who are of the day be sober, putting on the breastplate of faith and love, and as a helmet the hope of salvation.*

Spiritual warfare is a reality. The truth is that God never intended for us to do battle with Satan without armor. In Ephesians 6 Paul paints an external word picture of the internal. The order in which Paul lists the Christian's armor is the same order with which a Roman soldier put on his armor. Various authors separate the armor into interesting categories.

- Some say all six pieces of armor are defensive, including the sword, which is used to defend against attack.
- Others say Paul lists five pieces of defensive armor and one offensive weapon, the sword, which is used to attack the enemy.
- Some include prayer and even proclamation as pieces of the armor, while others do not.
- One says the belt and breastplate are foundational, the shoes and helmet are attached, and the shield and sword are movable.

In this chapter we will look at the first three pieces of armor, which a soldier put on; then, in the next chapter, we will look at the last three pieces of armor, which a solder picked up. Finally, we will consider prayer and proclamation as the purposeful activities to be carried out because of and beyond the equipping process.

If your faith consists of doing what comes naturally, feeling a few warm, fuzzy thoughts, or pondering an occasional noble religious sentiment, then you won't need this armor, since Satan likely is not threatened by you. Otherwise, read on! Some Christians like to "pray on their armor" every morning. I prefer never to take it off at night. Satan can do a world of damage during the night watches, especially if he finds us without our armor. When King David returned to his palace from a battle and took off his armor, he was in greater danger than when he was on the battlefield (2 Sam. 11). You say Roman soldiers didn't sleep in their armor. They did if the enemy was at the gate. If the enemy isn't bothering you, perhaps you don't need this armor after all. So, here are three pieces of armor to affirm daily but not remove nightly.

THE BELT THAT HOLDS EVERYTHING TOGETHER —TRUTHFULLY

By description, this was a leather, cloth, or metal belt that held all else together. It was crucial for the sword. Imagine a soldier reaching for his sword and it not being there.

I grew up watching Zorro on TV. When he got in a real bind, which he did approximately three times per weekly program, he would reach for his sword and cut a "Z" on someone's chest. What if Zorro reached for his sword and it was not there? A soldier must have confidence that the belt will hold the sword in place.

Becoming wider in the back, the belt offered support for the back to help keep a soldier from growing weary in the midst of the battle.

Gathering the robe and tucking it into the belt set a soldier free for movement. *"The truth shall set you free"* (John 8:32).

Others may grope about in lies, but Christians can move about more freely and quickly because they know the truth; it has set them free.

Our business in making disciples is to set people free from the bondage of sin. Truth will do that, because it set us free. Truth always wins. That's why I would rather side with the minority of people who base their lives on truth than with the majority who live in falsehood. It gives us a sense of support, lest we grow weary in the conflict.

Besides being a gathering place for the robe and a support for the back, the belt protected the *loins* (KJV), the lower half of the body, from injury. In an interesting parallel passage Peter says to *gird up the loins of your mind* (1 Pet. 1:13). This is a reference to the intellect or understanding. Therefore the thoughts, intentions, desires, and motives are included. The necessity of protecting them is emphasized.

The writer of Proverbs reminds us about man that *as he thinks in his heart, so is he* (Prov. 23:7). In the mind all virtue is first formed and all vice is first shaped. Every act is twice performed—once in the mind and once in the acting out of the mind's thoughts. The second performance is but a child of the first.

An old Latin proverb says, "Unless the vessel be clean, whatever you put into it turns sour." The mind must be protected with the *belt of truth*; otherwise, even the good ideas that travel our way will turn bad.

Scholars have viewed truth from two perspectives. First *truth* can mean God's truth. In other words it may mean Christian doctrine or the content of God's revelation through the Bible. Second, *truth* can be viewed as truthfulness of heart or purpose—sincerity or integrity. In all likelihood Paul is referring to both, since they are so tightly interrelated. God's truth would lead to personal truthfulness. All attempts at personal truthfulness ultimately fail unless they are based on God's truth.

Many would lead us astray in our thinking, apart from the truth. Post-modernism says no absolutes exist, but that statement is an absolute. Post-modernists say truth is relative, but we Christians know God's truth is unchanging. God's truth is not relative. Not everyone agrees with that.

The prayer was not eloquent. In it I had made reference to a quote that bothered the speaker of the day. This occurred at the graduation ceremony at the University of Texas; the Baptists' year to pray had arrived. So as the Baptist campus minister I was designated to offer this prayer. As we marched in, dressed in our academic colors, I was attracted to the words inscribed in marble over the doors to the main building. We would sit during the ceremony, just under that inscription, and face the students and guests seated on the lawn. The quote was from the Bible, *"And ye shall know the truth, and the truth shall make you free"* (John 8:32 KJV). My invocation seemed a fitting place to call attention to that quote. I had a feeling very few eyes were closed anyway. Then I thanked God for sending Jesus Christ—the truth—to set us free. The commencement speaker was president of a Southwest university noted for its academic standing and was, no doubt, an extremely well-educated man. I could tell that by his colors, since the colors on an academic robe represent various levels of achievement as well as signify disciplines of study. In his speech, just as most of the audience was falling asleep, this president turned to where I sat on the platform and said, "I must correct the Reverend Mr. Crawford's prayer of a few moments ago. Truth is relative! It is not embodied in any one person." I sat and smiled. I knew two things: 1. the Bible told me the speaker was mistaken, and 2. I had the benediction in which to make a rebuttal. Truth is not relative. It finds its best expression in the Person of Jesus Christ and suits us well as our first piece of armor.

So we sometimes sing the old German melody with the hymn text of Basil Manly, Jr.:

> Soldiers of Christ, in truth arrayed,
> A world in ruins needs your aid.

The truth that holds all else together offers support and protects the mind. These are targets that Satan loves to hit and does so with amazing frequency. So, work diligently to remain focused in your intercessory prayer for the truthful proclamation of the gospel.

DRESSED IN HIS RIGHTEOUSNESS

This piece of armor protected the vital organs, such as the lungs, the throat, and the heart—which biblical writers considered the center of emotions. It was made of small metal plates, overlapping each other like shield on shield and wrapping, to some extent, around the back, but not necessarily protecting the back. It was actually more like a coat or a vest put on backward than just a breastplate.

Righteousness offers protection for the Christian. Here, righteousness is understood in both of its New Testament meanings. God imputes righteousness to the nonbeliever when he or she believes in Christ. Thus, when Satan attacks me by bringing up my pre-Christian sins, I simply refer him to God's imputed righteousness.

The believer's personal, God-given righteousness results in moral uprightness and integrity. Paul reminds us that he does not possess his own righteousness (Phil. 3:9). When Satan attacks me with up-to-date temptations that challenge my uprightness and integrity, I simply refer him to the personal righteousness I possess in Christ.

Without righteousness the Christian is as vulnerable as is the opposition, but with righteousness we are protected. The psalmist wrote, *I have been young, and now am old; Yet I have not seen the righteous forsaken* (Ps. 37:25).

A man once accused Plato of crimes. Plato's response was, "We must live in such a way as to prove that his accusations are a lie." The paraphrase I offer seminary students is, "So live, that when rumors are surrounding you, no one will believe them."

On our televisions have we not seen images of people, perhaps patriotic souls, who have wrapped themselves in their country's flag to make some point? Here Paul is offering a similar image of wrapping righteousness around us as a "flag" or a coat.

What a picture—a leprous sinner, wearing the robe of Christ's righteousness. How can it be? This happens because:

• In my wrongness Christ died to make me right.
• In my disobedience Christ died to make me obedient.
• In my prodigal wanderings Christ lives to bring me back home to the Father.
• In my daily sinfulness, Christ lives to forgive and restore.

No wonder this piece of armor has leant itself to so much church music:

• Count Zinzendorf: *Jesus, Thy Blood and Righteousness—*
Jesus, Thy blood and righteousness
My beauty are, my glorious dress.

Midst flaming worlds, in these arrayed.
With joy shall I lift up my head.

• Edward Mote: *The Solid Rock—*
When He shall come with trumpet sound,
O may I then in Him be found,
Dressed in His righteousness alone
Faultless I stand before the throne.

Clothe yourself in both imputed and moral righteousness, without which you are very vulnerable to Satan's attacks. He loves to challenge our integrity and moral uprightness. So, dress up in righteousness and pray for the proclamation of the gospel.

GOSPEL SHOES OF PEACE
THAT DON'T FALL TO PIECES

My shoes, which wear out every few months, pale in comparison to God's shoes. In Deuteronomy 29:5 we read, *"And I have led you forty years in the wilderness. Your clothes have not worn out on you, and your sandals have not worn out on your feet."* How long can you wear a pair of shoes? God's shoes are adequate and eternal.

Here we have hobnail sandals, with spikes similar to modern track shoes or golf shoes. They were designed to keep the feet securely planted during hand-to-hand combat, no matter how sloped or slippery the ground on which the soldier stood. Consisting essentially of thick soles with straps, they were designed by Alexander the Great for quickness in battle. Some were made of leather, others of felt or cloth or even wood. A few were ornamented with lines of gold, silver, or silk, and occasionally were embroidered with jewels. They often were bound with iron as described in the Old Testament: *Your sandals shall be iron and bronze* (Deut. 33:25).

The roads were bad and often were built of large, sharp, uneven rocks. Briars and thorns were numerous. Stinging insects of various shapes and sizes were everywhere. Protection of the feet was of utmost importance.

A cruel method of warfare was to plant sharp, unseen sticks in the ground. It was the forerunner of modern land mines.

So Paul writes, *Shod your feet*—better translated, "bind the sandals under your feet."

Who can underestimate the importance of good shoes and their effect on the entire body?

Some have applied these gospel shoes to the Christian being quick to carry the gospel to others, and so he or she must (*"How beautiful are the feet of those who preach the gospel of peace . . ."*—Rom. 10:15). This is the very purpose of the ambassador; it is what gets Satan's attention and causes us to have to stand against him.

However the primary emphasis here is on defense in the midst of warfare—to stand firm against the enemy. *Readiness* used in the NIV and *preparation* used in other translations refer to being ready or prepared to take a stand and stand firm against the enemy, rather than being ready or prepared to advance the gospel.

Are you ready? Not if you have one foot in the world and the other in church. You'll surely slip and not stand. Paul writes, *let him who thinks he stands take heed lest he fall* (1 Cor. 10:12). Peter adds, *beware lest you also fall from your own steadfastness, being led away with the error of the wicked* (2 Pet. 3:17).

Satan is always lurking. False teachers are everywhere.

Nothing matters to Satan as long as he can get to us. Thus, we must know what we believe. One TV preacher said, "Just trust Jesus and everything will be OK." Some faithful saints would testify otherwise. I'm not OK. You're not OK. It's not OK. In fact we are standing against that which is not OK.

Martin Luther, facing 12 centuries of Roman Catholicism, said, "Here I stand. I can do no other." Likewise, we too stand in gospel shoes.

These are not just shoes but shoes of *peace*. Christian soldiers have a peace that passes understanding and that holds us secure in difficult times. Paul implies now that you possess God's peace; fight to defend it. A threefold peace exists:

- Peace with God wherein no doubting of our salvation occurs. *Therefore, having been justified by faith, we have peace with God through our Lord Jesus Christ* . . . (Rom. 5:1). Without assurance you are a casualty waiting to happen.
- Peace with self through which we concentrate on the battle, not on self. *Be anxious for nothing, but in everything by prayer and supplication, with thanksgiving, let your requests be made known to God; and the peace of God, which surpasses all understanding, will guard your hearts and minds through Jesus Christ* (Phil. 4:6-7).
- Peace with others without which jealously will destroy your focus. *If it is possible, as much as depends on you, live peaceably with all men* (Rom. 12:18).

Good shoes assist in defense. With adequate traction one is allowed to stand in the midst of the battle. In the Christian life nothing is more important than balance. The enemy loves to get us off balance. How can we be so relaxed under pressure? We do so because of an inner peace that passes understanding, just as hobnailed shoes allow one to relax in the midst of activity

Related to the shoes, you should have an adequate grasp on peace—with God, with others, and with self—that enables you to stand firm in defense against the attacks of the enemy as you pray for the proclamation of the gospel.

What to Do While Armed for Prayer and Proclamation

1. Gird up with truth that holds all else together, offers support, and protects the mind.
2. Get dressed in righteousness.
3. Put on gospel shoes that do not wear out in the midst of the conflict.

Questions for Reflection and/or Discussion

1. What does it mean for you or a friend to put on truth?
2. How would you or a friend look dressed in God's righteousness?
3. If you or a friend wore gospel shoes, what would this mean to you?

Chapter 8

FURTHER ARMED FOR PRAYER AND PROCLAMATION

above all, taking the shield of faith with which you will be able to quench all the fiery darts of the wicked one, and take the helmet of salvation, and the sword of the Spirit, which is the word of God

Let's put a parenthesis in the armor. A division occurs at the beginning of verse 16. *Above all* does not mean "more important than" but "in addition to." The first three pieces of armor were described as us *having* them. The second three pieces are described as us *taking* them. The first three pieces are attached. The second three are taken up and set down. The first three pieces are passive. The second three are active.

If you insist on "praying on your armor daily", you can pray on these three pieces while you affirm the previous three, which never should have been removed. Even with the enemy near, the soldier might sleep with his shield, his helmet, and his sword nearby.

A DARTBOARD IN THE SHAPE OF A SHIELD

In almost every family's photo album is a picture of a child dressed in his or her parents' clothing and dreaming of the day when adult clothes will fit. It is a humorous yet somewhat pathetic scene. A similar Old Testament picture occurs of David dressed in Saul's armor to face Goliath. Soldiers of that day believed being dressed in armor was the only way to resist and fight the enemy. But Saul's armor was too large and bulky for David. So David went instead with only his slingshot. Actually, David went armed with God's armor; with it he was invincible. The world dresses us in its armor and says this is the way it should be. Since God never intended his followers to stand ill-equipped or unequipped before Satan, He inspired Paul to give us in Ephesians 6 a description of spiritual armor. We have seen the belt, the breastplate, and the shoes. Now we look at the shield, a picture that on the surface looks as humorous as a child in adult clothes.

Paul is not referring to a small, round shield but to a large shield the size of a door. The shield was made of alternating layers of bronze and oxhide—truly fireproof. In fact, the Greek word for *shield* is the same Greek word translated *door.*

The small shield was carried when no fierce battle was raging, but when a battle was to occur, soldiers carried the large shields. The enemy arrows—*fiery darts* dipped in pitch or some other combustible material and set afire—were the reason for shields of this size. It was one of the most devastating weapons of ancient warfare. These *fiery darts* were the predecessors of today's incendiary bombs. The psalmist refers to the making of *arrows into fiery shafts*, (Ps. 7:13) and *Sharp arrows of the warrior, with coals of the broom tree!* (Ps. 120:4).

Herodotus mentions the fact that in ancient warfare, one customarily fixed pieces of tow (broken fibers of plant stalks reduced to the substance needed for spinning) to the arrows, dipped them in pitch, set them afire, and sent them on their way, at random, toward the enemy.

By the way Paul believed in a personal devil. Do you?

Paul was affirmed by Peter—*Beloved, do not think it strange concerning the fiery trial which is to try you* . . . (1 Pet. 4:12) and by John—*the whole world lies under the sway of the wicked one* (1 John 5:19).

John Bunyan, in *Pilgrim's Progress*, makes use of the satanic image in a very graphic description of Christian with Apollyon.

One day Martin Luther, while working at his desk in Wartburg Castle in Eisenach, Germany, saw Satan as so real that Luther threw the inkpot at Satan. The stain remained on the wall for years. I've been to this spot in Germany; guides point to the stain—or perhaps the place where the original stain has been enhanced for tourism.

Paul conceives of a real Satan as the one who fires burning arrows at Christians and Christians as defending themselves with faith. This is the air attack preceding the ground attack of face-to-face combat. It is designed to soften the enemy. But no matter how intense Satan's temptations may become, faith will cause them to fall to the ground like broken arrows, spent and ineffective.

Faith in God is a comprehensive protection against all of the flaming temptations that Satan may hurl at us:

- The arrow of pride, which gives birth to self-love and self-advancement to the determent of the group.
- The arrow of envy, leading to jealousy which destroys families as well as fraternal relationships. The story of Cinderella and her jealous stepsisters never has needed a commentary to explain its meaning.
- The arrow of evil passion, which arouses every degrading desire of human nature and causes disease, misery, sorrow, and even premature death.
- The arrow of doubt, which leads believers into uncer-

tainty and distracts the mind from truth.

The solution is unflinching, unfaltering, unflappable faith—faith that includes what you believe and how you live. Faith never stops with the intellectual but always includes the practical. James reminds us, *faith without works is dead* (Jas. 2:20). Peter reminds us to *Resist him, steadfast in the faith* . . . (1 Pet. 5:9). John reminds us faith *is the victory that has overcome the world* . . . (1 John 5:4).

A fine line exists between faith and foolishness. Often you cannot, until after the fact, completely distinguish the difference between the two. What the believer sees as faith, the nonbeliever often sees as foolishness.

Faith has always looked foolish to those who don't have any. That's why they laughed at Abraham, Noah, David (*the Lord God is a* . . . *shield*—Ps. 84:11), and Paul (*We are fools for Christ's sake* . . . —1 Cor. 4:10).

But faith protects. It brings God in between us and the enemy just as the shield is placed between the soldier and the arrow.

The corporate advantage was seen as soldiers marched shield to shield so no dart could penetrate the ranks. If one soldier dropped his shield, a fiery dart could get behind the lines and do devastating, widespread damage. The circumstances of our times call for believers to close the ranks.

With both the personal and the corporate application Paul is saying that faith should accomplish two purposes: 1. defend us personally from Satan's fiery darts, and 2. link us with others of the faith in a way so as to present a solid wall of defense against the enemy.

The essence of preparation related to the door-sized shield was adequate faith-protection against the *fiery darts* of Satan. As we stand together, shield to shield, we resist Satan's attack on the body of Christ, the church, and our intercession for the proclamation of the gospel.

LEADING WITH YOUR HEAD . . . WHILE YOU WEAR THE RIGHT HELMET

The phrase *leading with your head* refers to thinking ahead and calculating the possibilities before taking action. It often is used in contrast to leading with your heart, which refers to leading with emotions rather than reason. While not neglecting the importance of emotions, Paul here wants to be sure that his readers understood the importance of protecting the head.

The helmet protected the head and the mind. It was made of leather or perhaps of metal. It was somewhat like a close-fitting skullcap. Most helmets included plates to protect the cheeks, a band for the forehead, and a collar-like projection to protect the back of the neck. Such a helmet, when closed, exposed little other than the eyes, nose, and mouth.

Here Paul describes it as the *helmet of salvation*, while in another place he refers to it is as *a helmet the hope of salvation* (1 Thess. 5:8). Rather than being a contradiction, this fits Paul's theology that salvation is past, present, and future—we were saved, we are being saved, we shall be saved (justification, sanctification, and glorification). Thus it is both a helmet of present-tense salvation and a helmet of the future hope of salvation.

The term *of salvation* seems somewhat strange, since we normally think of salvation related to the heart, not the head. Yet Paul wrote in Romans *be transformed by the renewing of your mind* . . . (Rom. 12:2). Satan wants to attack your mind as he did with Eve (Gen. 3:2, 2 Cor. 11:1-3).

The head entered the conversation between God and Satan about Job. God finally relented and allowed Satan to tempt Job. Satan took Job's camels, sheep, other livestock, and even his children, yet Job did not curse God. Another conversation between God and Satan allowed Satan to maintain that Job was faithful because he was not allowed to be touched personally. At that point, *And the Lord said to Satan, "Behold, he is in your hand, but spare his life"* (Job 2:6). But the same Hebrew word translated "life" is also translated "mind" or "reason". As long as Job had his right mind—his ability to reason, he would not forsake God in spite of Satan's attack.

Is Satan playing mind games with you as he did with Job? Remember your salvation. You were instructed to *take* it as a gift—the gift of salvation. The Greek word here is different from either of the ones used earlier—*take up*. All other armor is to be picked up or put on, but the helmet of salvation is to be taken as one would *take* a gift. Indeed, salvation is *the gift of God* (Eph. 2:8).

Interestingly enough, even the Lord wears this helmet—He doesn't need it, but He wears it. Jesus didn't need baptism either but did it as an example. Isaiah 59:17 says, *For He put on righteousness as a breastplate, and a helmet of salvation on His head.* If Jesus, who did not need this armor, saw fit nevertheless to wear it, how much more should we be equipped with it?

Here is the assurance of past and present salvation as well as the hope of future salvation as it secures our stance against Satanic attack. Satan may play with our minds, but he can no more win us over than he could win over Job.

A SWORD THAT ASSISTS BOTH WAYS— OFFENSIVELY AND DEFENSIVELY

Now we arrive at the only piece of offensive armor and the only piece needed. The sword always has been a formidable weapon of warfare. The earliest swords were made of flint; then the bronze swords arrived on the scene, followed by the

Egyptian swords of iron and the still-later steel swords. Some were two-edged, with the points turned outward, so as to tear a man to pieces on removing the sword from his body.

A possible misinterpretation occurs here. The phrase *the sword of the Spirit, which is the Word of God* leads one to believe the Spirit is the Word of God. Nowhere in the Bible is this true. Correctly the phrase reads *Take the sword which the Spirit Himself provides for you.*

It might also help to realize that the Greek word used for *word* in this verse is not the common word, *logos*, but the less-common word, *rhema*. *Logos* when used in the New Testament refers to Jesus Christ, the Word that was *with God* and *was God* (John 1:1) and the Word that *became flesh* (John 1:14). The Bible, which is the written Word of God, informs us about Jesus. *Rhema* means a saying or a word spoken.

The comparison of the sword to speech was frequent in the Old Testament:

- *Whose teeth are spears and arrows, and their tongue a sharp sword* (Ps. 57:4)
- *sharpen their tongue like a sword* (Ps. 64:3)
- *He has made My mouth like a sharp sword* (Isa. 49:2)

Literally, the *word* means "the thing said" and refers to the utterances of God, which include but are not limited to the Bible. When Paul wrote this letter, much of the Bible was not yet written or assembled. God was, in fact, still speaking in the time Paul wrote this. Some believe this was a reference to the Word of God being preached. While that is also a possibility, the primary application of this phrase is to the Bible. We sing about :

Standing on the promises of Christ the Lord
Bound to Him eternally by love's strong cord,
Overcoming daily with the Spirit's sword,
Standing on the promises of God.

Three contrasts are used:

- *Sword of the Spirit* was probably used in contrast to the famous Damascus steel of the day. Soldiers would brag of their sword that it was a "sword of Damascus". Paul says this is a *sword of the Spirit*.
- While leaders of other world religions have taught that their religion advances with the use of a physical sword, Paul is teaching that the Christian faith moves forward with the *sword of the Spirit*.
- The book of Revelation pictures Jesus destroying His enemies with a sword in His mouth (Rev. 19:15, 21). This implies that His victory and ours shall be won by the *sword of the Spirit*.

The bottom line is that we are not to fight Satan alone—in our own strength, ideas, and power. We are to fight him with the Word, which the very Spirit of God has produced.

Knowing the contents of the Bible is one thing; altogether different is knowing how to use the Bible correctly. This is best illustrated in the temptation experience of Jesus. Three times Satan approaches Jesus with temptation (Luke 4). Just as Jesus used the Word as a threefold defense during His temptation experience in the wilderness (Deut. 8:3; 6:16; 6:13), so must we be ready to use the Word, both in our defense of the gospel and in our offense against Satan—even to the point that Satan leaves Jesus alone—*for a season.* James said, if you resist him, he will flee from you.

Practically speaking then, we can do six things with our sword-Bible.

Hear the Bible
- Romans 10:17—*Faith comes by hearing, and hearing by the word of God.*
- Revelation 1:3—*Blessed is he who reads and those who hear the words of this prophecy.*

Read the Bible
- 1 Peter 2:2—*as newborn babes, desire the pure milk of the word, that you may grow thereby.*
- 1 Timothy 4:13—*Till I come, give attention to reading, to exhortation, to doctrine.*

Study the Bible
- 2 Timothy 2:15—*Study to shew thyself approved unto God, a workman that needeth not to be ashamed, rightly dividing the word of truth.* (KJV)
- Acts 17:11—*they received the word with all readiness, and searched the Scriptures daily . . ..*
- John 5:39—*You search the Scriptures, for in them you think you have eternal life; and these are they which testify of Me.*

Meditate on the Bible
- 1 Timothy 4:15—*Meditate on these things.*
- Luke 2:19—*But Mary kept all these things and pondered* (meditated on) *them in her heart.*

Memorize the Bible
- Psalm 119:11—*Your word have I hidden in my heart That I might not sin against You.*

Apply the Bible

- James 1:22—*But be doers of the word, and not hearers only . . ..*
- Matthew 7:24—*"Therefore whoever hears these words of Mine and does them, I will liken him to a wise man who built his house on the rock . . .."*

A final observation is in order. Paul describes no armor for the back. Nor did the Roman soldier have any such armor. For the Roman soldier as well as for the Christian soldier, no occasion for retreat—for turning back—existed. In the words of Charles Wesley:

> Soldiers of Christ, arise,
> And put your armor on,
> Strong in the strength which God supplies
> Through His eternal Son.

So, the final piece of armor is the offensive weapon—the Word of God—which is to be heard, read, studied, meditated on, memorized, and applied. When used properly in combination with the five pieces of defensive armor no need occurs for armor protecting the back.

Therefore, we can pray for the proclamation of the gospel while we are fully armed against Satan's attacks.

What to Do to While Armed for Prayer and Proclamation

1. Take up your shield to quench the fiery darts of Satan.
2. Take salvation and cover your head with it.
3. Draw swords.

Questions for Reflection and/or Discussion

1. How much faith would you or a friend need to actually take up the shield of faith?

2. If salvation were a helmet for you or a friend, what would this mean?

3. How could you or a friend more effectively use the sword of the Spirit, the Bible?

Chapter 9

ADVANCING THROUGH PRAYER AND PROCLAMATION

praying always . . .
that utterance may be given . . .
that I may speak boldly

Having explored the six pieces of spiritual armor, we now turn to Paul's personal requests. Apparently these are not additional pieces of armor, as no part of the body is mentioned. Previously, Paul has carefully followed the armor of the Roman soldier. Here he diverts to discuss reasons for needing all of this armor.

Various scholars through the years have noted the relationship of the spiritual armor in verses 10-17 to the activities of prayer and proclamation in verses 18-20.

Charles Hodge writes in *The Crossway Classic Commentaries*:

> It is not armor or weapons which make the warrior. There must be courage and strength—and even then he often needs help. As the Christian has no resources of strength in himself and can succeed only as helped from above, the apostle

urges the duty of prayer . . . This verse is linked with "stand firm then" in verse 14: "Stand, therefore, with all kinds of prayers and requests. Pray in the Spirit on all occasions."[1]

Francis Foulkes writes in *The Tyndale New Testament Commentaries*:

> Prayer cannot quite be described as a part of the armor, but the description of the Christian's equipment for the conflict cannot but include reference to prayer . . .. The Greek has a participle "praying", which may in fact be taken with all the foregoing commands. The different parts of the armor have been described, and in effect the apostle would say, "Each piece put on with prayer."[2]

James Montgomery Boice believes:

> You and I can be clothed in God's armor—having the belt of truth, the breastplate of righteousness, our feet shod with the readiness that come from the gospel of peace, the shield of faith, the helmet of salvation, and the sword of the Spirit—and yet fail to triumph because we do not call upon God.[3]

John R.W. Stott concludes:

> Finally, Paul adds prayer, not because he thinks of prayer as another unnamed weapon, but because it is to pervade all our spiritual warfare.

Equipping ourselves with God's armor is not a mechanical operation; it is itself an expression of our dependence on God, in other words of prayer.[4]

Long before modern warfare Paul understood the fact that two targets must be destroyed if an army wished to win a battle. In every recent war the winning side has attacked the enemy's ability to communicate and its ability to attack, or better phrased, its offense.

When Satan goes on the attack against Christians, he first attacks our prayer lives (communication) and our ability to proclaim the gospel (offense). So Paul is absolutely correct in first asking for the intercessory prayer support of his readers and then discussing the proclamation of the gospel.

praying always with all prayer and supplication in the Spirit, being watchful to this end with all perseverance and supplication for all the saints —and for me, that utterance may be given to me, that I may open my mouth boldly to make known the mystery of the gospel, for which I am an ambassador in chains; that I may speak boldly, as I ought to speak (Eph. 6:18-20).

BEYOND ARMOR — PRAYER

In the midst of the conflict, occasions arise in which we must set aside the sword and communicate with the Commander-in-Chief. Thus Paul writes of *praying always*.

This follows the model of Jesus, who instructed His disciples in Gethsemane, during His most intense spiritual struggle,

to *watch and pray lest you enter into temptation* (Mark 14:38).
Warren W. Wiersbe reminds us to:

> Pray with your eyes open. "Watching" means
> "keeping on the alert." The phrase "watch and
> pray" occurs often in the Bible. When
> Nehemiah was repairing the walls of Jerusalem,
> and the enemy was trying to stop the work,
> Nehemiah defeated the enemy by watching and
> praying. "Nevertheless we made our prayer
> unto God, and set a watch" (Neh. 4:9). "Watch
> and pray" is the secret of victory over the world
> (Mark 13:33), the flesh (Mark 14:38), and the
> devil (Eph. 6:18). Peter went to sleep when he
> should have been praying, and the result was a
> victory for Satan (Mark 14:29-31, 67-72). God
> expects us to use our God-given senses, led by
> the Spirit, so that we detect Satan when he is
> beginning to work.[5]

Remember John Bunyan's account in *Pilgrim's Progress*?
In the middle of the Valley of the Shadow of Death, Christian
discovers a place he believes to be "the mouth of hell."
Bunyan writes:

> And ever and anon the flame and smoke would
> come out in such abundance with sparks and
> hideous noises, (things that cared not for
> Christian's sword, as did Apollyon before,) that
> he was forced to put up his sword, and betake
> himself to another weapon, called *all prayer.*[6]

Bunyan continued to write that when Christian wielded this

mighty weapon of prayer, the demons of Hell "gave back, and came no farther."[7]

In his companion letter to the church at Colossae, Paul wrote similar words, *praying also for us, that God would open to us a door for the word, to speak the mystery of Christ, for which I am also in chains* (Col. 4:3).

Paul's statement *with all prayer* is an all-inclusive phrase that includes the act of worship. He uses the same order *prayer and supplication* elsewhere. *Be anxious for nothing, but in everything by prayer and supplication . . . let your requests be made known to God* (Phil. 4:6).

Supplication is a more narrow word than *prayer*. We supplicate for things. We petition for self. We intercede for others. However, the lines that divide these words often are fuzzy. Occasionally an overlap of meanings occurs, as is the case here. Paul is asking for *supplication* for *all the saints*. We might call it *intercession* for all the saints in today's terminology. The truth is, when the battle rages, more people are affected than just those in the midst of the fighting—*all the saints*.

This supplication was to *persevere*—the direct opposite of growing tired and giving up in the midst of the battle. We are never to allow ourselves to grow slack in our prayer life but always to remain near the presence of God, so that at any moment communication can take place.

So Paul's prayer request indicates prayer should be:

- Continual—*praying always*
- Intense—*with all perseverance*
- Comprehensive—*for all the saints*

The emphasis on prayer underlines a priority of the Christian life. Indeed, the spiritual armor cannot be used except in relation to our communication with God.

Communication with God is a priority. A powerful, satanic temptation is to make us think that once we have put on our armor we are safe. Armor, of itself, will not fully protect us from the enemy. Armor, plus communication with God, will better protect us from the enemy.

Praying *in the Spirit* allows the Holy Spirit to take over your prayer agenda. This is more than ritualistic prayer, more than formal prayer, more than proper posture in prayer, more than the correct words used in prayer, more than "vain repetitions" in prayer, and more than your planned time for prayer. In this kind of praying the Spirit often impresses on our minds items for which and persons for whom we have not previously planned to include in our prayers. Yielding to this prompting of the Spirit allows us to pray in sync with the Father's will.

As we pray like this, we are doing so in the line of great prayer warriors of the past.

- Abraham took 318 trained servants and through prayer conquered a coalition of kings (Gen. 14).
- Gideon reduced his army from 32,000 to 300 and through prayer delivered Israel from slavery.
- Joshua through prayer defeated Jericho against great odds (Josh. 6).
- Jesus through prayer battled Satan in Gethsemane.
- Paul, while in prison, with prayer engaged Satan.
- John with prayer confronted Satan from Patmos.

A more recent prayer warrior has been identified by Hudson Taylor. During the days of the China Inland Mission one station attracted a lot of attention. Both the number of spiritual converts and their spiritual development far exceeded that of the other stations. The consecration of the missionaries at the other stations was just as great; their work ethic was just as intense. Then Hudson Taylor visited England. At the close of one speaking engagement a man approached him and introduced himself. As they talked, Taylor clearly saw that the man knew a great deal about this particular station in which the number of converts was so great. When Taylor asked the man about it, he replied, "The missionary there and I are old college friends. He sends me names of enquirers and converts and I daily take these names to God in prayer." At last, the secret was discovered: an intercessor, praying daily, for specific requests produced a mission station experiencing exceptional results.

So how does prayer relate to spiritual warfare? In their book *Power House: A Step-by-Step Guide to Building a Church that Prays*, Glen Martin and Dian Ginter offer a step-by-step path that leads prayer into spiritual warfare:

1. Introduction is the level of prayer in which a believer first begins to realize that personally talking with God about matters of concern is possible.
2. Initiation takes place as the believer reaches out beyond and broadens self-centered praying to include a wider scope of requests, such as family and close friends.
3. Imitation is when the believer becomes more aware of how others are praying and begins to learn from them.
4. Intercession is implemented when the believer has more of a burden that drives toward prayer for others.
5. Investigation causes faith to increase as the believer begins to believe in a God who can and will do what is requested in prayer.
6. Invasion is when the believer operates on a level of prayer that "attacks the gates of the enemy." At this

point, the term *spiritual warfare* is often heard and used.[8]

As the conflict rages, our assignments are to intercede to God for each other—and especially for those who are caught in the crossfire of the battle's front lines.

BEYOND ARMOR—PROCLAMATION

Having successfully armed ourselves and being ready to intercede, we now hear Paul requesting prayer for himself. The object of his prayer was for bold utterance (proclamation) of the gospel. He well understood that evangelism involves simply collecting the spoils of victories won in prayer. A person should never talk to people about God until that person has first talked to God about the people. Thus, in proper order, Paul writes of prayer and then proclamation.

This was not Paul's only request for prayer. He also asks the believers in Colossae (Col. 4:3) to pray for him. Likewise he asks the believers in Thessalonica (1 Thess. 5:25; 2 Thess. 3:1) to remember him before God. He understood the absolute necessity of being remembered in prayer.

When Paul wrote the word *utterance*, he was a prisoner, but he did not ask prayer for release. He was a sick man, but he did not ask prayer for healing. He was less concerned that his chains be loosed than he was that his mouth be opened— not that he be set free, but that the gospel would spread freely. So, offering a point to their prayer, he asked prayer for his verbal witness—his proclamation.

Satan dislikes few things more than the verbal proclamation of the gospel. Yet we have many excuses for not proclaiming the gospel:

- "My life is my witness"—only if nonbelievers know who you are. Otherwise, your life witness is not much of a threat to Satan.
- "I am a faithful church member." Satan doesn't worry much about church attendance. Your neighbors and friends expect church attendance of you. But when we aggressively begin to attempt to persuade Satan's folks to move their membership into God's kingdom, Satan gets upset.
- "I'm not a good speaker." We forget that Paul was not a polished speaker. Some at Corinth had taunted him about his *"contemptible"* speech (2 Cor. 10:10). He was overshadowed in oratory by Apollos, so he asks for help in his proclamation.

In the parallel passage of Colossians 4:3 Paul asked specifically that his readers pray that *God would open to us a door for the word, to speak the mystery of Christ, for which I am also in chains.*

Then Paul asks for *boldness* in his presentation of the gospel. In Acts 4:13, 29, 31 the same Greek word is translated "clarity." Those who are bold are often misunderstood. Those who are clear often lack zeal. This word calls for a blend of boldness and clarity in the proclamation of the gospel.

In our admiration of the missionary activities of Paul, we sometimes forget that he was not a polished orator. In fact the believers in Corinth said of him, *"his bodily presence is weak, and his speech contemptible"* (2 Cor. 10:10). Therefore, his prayer request for bold speech is all the more to be noted.

That which Paul wished to proclaim was *the mystery of the Gospel.* Paul lived in a day in which secret codes were popular for tight-knit organizations. In some cases, to reveal the code was punishable by death. So he captures the curiosity of his readers by mentioning a *mystery*. In Romans Paul had referred to *the mystery kept secret since the world began but now made manifest* (Rom. 16:25-26). The gospel mystery was that God in Christ had provided redemption for all persons. *God was in Christ reconciling the world to Himself . . .* (2 Cor. 5:19).

Finally, Paul identifies himself as an *ambassador*. An ambassador is one who represents his king in another kingdom. Words written many years ago by E.T. Cassell are appropriate here:

> I am a stranger here, within a foreign land;
> My home is far away, upon a golden strand;
> Ambassador to be of realms beyond the sea,
> I'm here on business for my King.
>
> This is the message that I bring,
> A message angles fain would sing:
> "O be ye reconciled." Thus saith my God and King,
> "O be ye reconciled to God."

As ambassadors, not secret agents, we should pray that in our own proclamation of the Gospel:

- we would be delivered from a spirit of compromise.
- we would not be guided by a spirit of diplomacy or expediency.
- we would be delivered from a spirit of fear.
- we would put the truth first and speak it with boldness.
- we would blend out boldness with a spirit of love, mercy, and compassion.

In the little East Texas church in which I served as pastor during my seminary student days, we often sang words seldom heard these days—but these are often needed today. Until recently I knew nothing of the background of the author. Her name is listed in the hymnbooks only as "Mrs. C. H. Morris." Research found that her name was actually Lelia Morris, a Methodist hymnwriter around the turn of the 20th century. In 1913 her eyesight failed; her son put up a 28-foot blackboard with staff-lines so she could continue to write her music. In spite of this challenge, which Satan no doubt tried to use to discourage her, Lelia Morris wrote:

The fight is on Oh Christian soldier and face to face
in stern array
With armor gleaming and colors streaming,
The right and wrong engage today.

The fight is on but be not weary. Be strong and
in His might hold fast.
If God be for us, His banner o're us.
We'll sing the victor's song at last.

In a battle that had gone bad, the general asked the private to sound the retreat, to which the private replied, "I don't know that tune, sir."

After several exchanges the private confessed, "Napoleon never taught me that tune"

"Then play something," shouted the angry general.

The young soldier sounded the "Charge". Soldiers all over the battlefield summoned new energy and turned the tide of the battle.

Let us not be content with putting on or praying on our armor while we ignore Paul's admonition to pray and proclaim. Every so often, someone needs to sound the "Charge."

What to Advance through Prayer and Proclamation

1. Advance with prayer for the proclamation of the gospel.
2. Pray for *all the saints*, even the ones you don't know or don't like.
3. Pray *boldly* for the bold proclamation of the gospel.

Questions for Reflection and/or Discussion

1. Are you hearing the sound of the retreat or the sound of the charge?
2. What could you or a friend do tomorrow to pray more effectively?
3. What could you or a friend do tomorrow to more effectively proclaim the gospel?

[1] Alister McGrath, and J.I. Packer, Senior Editors. *The Crossway Classic Commentaries.* "*Ephesians*" by Charles Hodge. Wheaton, IL, and Nottingham, England: Crossway Books, 1994, p. 220.

[2] Leon Morris, Editor. *The Tyndale New Testament Commentaries.* "Ephesians" by Francis Foulkes. Downers Grove, IL, and Nottingham, England: InterVarsity Press, 1989, p. 184.

[3] James Montgomery Boice, *Ephesians; An Expositional Commentary.* Grand Rapids: Baker Books, 1988, 1997, p. 260.

[4] John R.W. Stott, *The Message of Ephesians.* Downers Grove, IL: InterVarsity Press, 1979, p. 283.

[5] Warren W. Wiersbe, *Be Rich: Gaining the Things that Money Can't Buy.* Colorado Springs: David C. Cook, 1979, p. 173.

[6] John Bunyan, *The Complete Works of John Bunyan: Pilgrim's Progress.* Philadelphia: Bradley, Garrison & Co., 1873, p. 119.

[7] Ibid, p. 119.

[8] Martin, Glen and Ginter, Dian. *Power House: A Step-by-Step Guide to Building a Church that Prays.* Nashville: Broadman & Holman Publishers, 1994, pp. 97-107.

CONCLUSION

What is important is not so much who you are but whose you are; not so much where you are but why; not so much your circumstances but what you do with them.

Someday, our last skirmish with Satan will be ended. We will have:

- Exhausted our empowering
- Shed our equipping
- Surrendered our position
- Resisted Satan's strategies
- Defended ourselves against the opposition
- Worn out our armor
- Removed our belt and breastplate
- Set aside our shoes and shield
- Laid down our helmet and sword
- Voiced our last prayer
- Uttered our last proclamation

Then a crown awaits.

'Ner think the battle won, nor lay your armor down.
The work of faith will not be done, till you obtain the crown.

The chaplain's flag had flown on his jeep during World War II. Its presence draped over his casket was more than symbolic. For more than 65 years of vocational ministry Edwin Crawford was a faithful disciple. Still speaking in churches six weeks before his cancer-induced death, he fought the good fight all the way to the end. He finished his course. So full and complete was his life that on the day of his death, all he had to do was die. Like the faithful servant in the parable of Jesus he heard his *"Well done, good and faithful servant . . . "* (Mt. 25:21), not because it was a routine heavenly welcome, but because he was a good and faithful servant who had done well. In heaven a crown awaited him—as do ones for you and for me—when the battle is over.

As we receive our crowns, the words of Janet Paschal could be sung for us, even as they were sung at my father's funeral.

His back is bent and weary
His voice is tired and low
His sword is worn from battle
And his steps have gotten slow
But he used to walk on water
Or it seemed that way to me
I know he moved some mountains
And never left his knees

He faced the winds of sorrow
But his heart knew no retreat
He walked in narrow places
Knowing Christ knew no defeat
But now his steps turn homeward
So much closer to the prize
He's sounding kind of homesick
And there's a longing in his eyes

Strike up the band
Assemble the choir

Another soldier's coming home
Another warrior hears the call he's waited for so long
He'll battle no more
But he's won his wars
Make sure heaven's table has room for one more
Sing a welcome song
Another soldier's coming home.[1]

[1]Janet Paschal, "Another Soldier's Coming Home." Maplesong Music. BMM Music (ASCAP), 1997. Used by permission.

Order more books by Dr. Dan Crawford

Ambassadors on Mission: The Priority of Prayer and Proclamation, by Dr. Dan Crawford. If you enjoyed this book, share it with your friends and loved ones. They will enjoy it as much as you have.

_____ **Copies at $14.95 =** _____

Mud Hen in a Peacock Parade by Dr. Dan Crawford. Go ahead and laugh. Jesus did. That's what you will do while reading this book. The author tells about church events, church people, and church leaders in a way that helps you see the humor instead of all the seriousness..

_____ **Copies at $14.95=** _____

God's Formula for Genuine Happiness by Dr. Dan Crawford. Have you ever wondered how happy you really are? Questioned what it means to be genuinely happy? Or thought about exactly what you'd need in order to feel that way? Whatever you think of your current degree of happiness, you'll be encouraged by the simple, profound truths waiting within this book.

_____ **Copies at $12.95=** _____

Add $4.00 postage and handling for first book, $1.00 for each additional book.

Shipping & Handling: _____
TX residents add 8.25% sales tax: _____

Total _____
(paid by check or money order) _____

Or pay by credit card (American Express, Discover, Visa, or MasterCard: credit card number _____
expiration date: _____ Signature: _____

Name: _____
Address_____
City_____State_____Zip _____
Phone _____ Email _____

See address and other contact information on page 123.

LaVergne, TN USA
24 January 2010
170991LV00002B/4/P